INTERNATIONAL BESTSELLER

CLARITY IS POWER

HOW TO STOP COMPARING AND
STEP INTO YOUR PERSONAL AUTHORITY

R U T H . S A W

Published in 2020 by The Clarity Expert
Publisher Registration No.: R2020042400001
www.theclarityexpert.co

ISBN 9789811460333 (Hardback)
ISBN 9789811460340 (Paperback)
ISBN 9789811460326 (E-book)

A catalogue record for this book is available from the National Library of Singapore

Cover design & illustrations by Rosalyn Ng
Photography by Cheeky Motion
Book layout & illustrations by Marvin Tojos
Editing by Linda Beaulieu and David Saw

In loving memory of Ting Poh Geok, my nanny, whom I consider my second mum, as well as David Bradshaw, my mentor and inspiration.

CLARITY IS PERSONAL

"We all need to see an optometrist to have a suitable pair of glasses prescribed to us for clear vision. Likewise, we all have different prescriptions and journeys to clarity.

I hope this book will provide you with practical tools and insights necessary for greater clarity in your own personal journey."

Your clarity optometrist,
Ruth Saw

"知己，知比，
百战百胜"
孙子兵法

.

DIRECT TRANSLATION

"KNOW YOURSELF,
KNOW YOUR OPPONENT,
A HUNDRED BATTLES,
A HUNDRED VICTORIES"

Sun Tzu, The Art of War
(written approx. 500 BCE)

Contents

Introduction 9

Chapter 1: Clarity is Power 17

Chapter 2: The 3W framework 35

Chapter 3: Staircase to Authority 75

Chapter 4: Clarity of Self 89

Chapter 5: Clarity of Others 125

Chapter 6: Clarity of Action 139

Chapter 7: The Most Important Battle 169

Spiritual Clarity 179

About the Author. 183

Acknowledgements. 185

About the publisher, The Clarity Expert 187

Introduction

---

*"Know yourself, know your opponent,
a hundred battles, a hundred victories"*
Sun Tzu, The Art of War

In this fast-paced world, especially with the explosion of social media, it's hard not to compare, isn't it? We look at Instagram and we see someone's beautiful life, and we wonder why ours doesn't look like that. Or we get stuck as we are bombarded with various choices available by our friends on social media. Or sometimes, we find ourselves doing things based on peer pressure, but not feeling satisfied.

A reporter was interviewing a 104-year-old woman for their newspaper. "So, what do you think is the best thing about being 104?" the reporter asked. She shrugged with a smile and simply replied, "No peer pressure!"

No one likes peer pressure and it's not necessary if you know what you want. It is never too late, and it does not depend on when and where you start. The sooner you find clarity of who you are, the sooner you'll be free from comparison. You don't have to wait till you are 104!

Stop comparing yourself with others. It doesn't build you. Rather, seek to be comfortable in your own skin.

As a strengths coach, I help others find clarity by showing them how they are uniquely wired and who they can be. True clarity comes from understanding who we are. But it doesn't stop there. To have absolute clarity means we can become what we see. It is not just a fantasy or dream. What we see clearly can become our reality.

Have you ever wondered, deep in your heart, if there is more to you and your life? Especially in times of uncertainty, when your identity seems shaken, do you stop and ask, "Who am I?" What is it that you really want for your life? Do you ever hope to step up into a bigger authority with strength and confidence?

Regardless of what we do, if we want to be the best we can be, we cannot escape from having to step up, whether it's for the next job interview, the next sale, or even the next business venture.

Maybe you've stopped believing there is more because when you start sharing your dreams with others, you get conflicting feedback. Or perhaps, you may have compared yourself with friends around you and felt that you fall short. Or maybe you've been living your life seeking to please others and meet their demands, but you feel unfulfilled. These may have left you feeling confused, inferior, immobilised, or worst of all, indifferent.

I have found that the key to greater authority starts with CLARITY. It is essential to have absolute clarity on who we are. Only then can we be free from confusion from the different opinions we receive. It will free us from comparing ourselves with others. We start being someone who can stand in our own conviction and authority. This is where we can influence at a greater level. Confidence, like authority, comes after clarity.

The good news is, with proper time and investment on yourself, you can find clarity and step into your personal authority with strength and confidence. Imagine yourself climbing a hill. The start may be tough. All you see is the step ahead of you. But there will come a time when you reach higher, and you can see clearer and further. Although it takes effort to step up, ironically life becomes more effortless when we are in our authority, for we can see clearer and further when we are higher. Our lives unfold into greater clarity with each step we take. You will find that in no time, you can influence with ease – because with greater clarity comes greater authority!

The key to battle success, according to the famous military strategist Sun Tzu in China (500 BCE), is to "know yourself and know your opponent, a hundred battles, a hundred victories." Back then, Sun Tzu was deployed by the emperor to help the city of Wu in China to fight against another city called Chu that was 10 times bigger. Logically, looking at the resources, it would be a war they could not win. However, Sun Tzu cleverly defeated the enemy and won the war. He penned down these strategies and it is known as *The Art of War*.

The Art of War strategies have been used in business schools and universities such as Yale, Harvard, Oxford, and mentioned in media worldwide. Sun Tzu's quote is so popular that it was used in the Hollywood movie, *Wall Street*, where Gordon Gecko used Sun Tzu's quote to coach Bud Fox!

In the context of influence, this same strategy can be applied to our personal victory. We all need to know ourselves and others, and craft effective battle plans, in order to step into our authority, which is our victory.

CLARITY is the future of authority. Authority will no longer be based on position or title. People will follow and trust someone who can lead with clarity, congruently from their heart. This is where you will become the best version of who you can be, for yourself and for those around you.

You may have heard this famous quote from Bill Gates:

> "Most people overestimate what they
> can do in one year and underestimate
> what they can do in ten years."

I'd like to encourage you to think way BIGGER for the long term. Take a moment now to pause and to take a deep breath and believe in yourself that there is a greater purpose for you to be here.

If you choose to believe in yourself, you will be guided through stories peppered in this book, with practical examples on how you can find clarity, and step into your personal and unique authority with strength and confidence.

Personally, I came to Australia in my mid 30s to do my MBA. The situation was not as I had expected. It took me over 6 months to find a job. I still remember I had to walk 45 minutes to my school just to save the $1.60 bus fare! Having tasted luxuries in life before (when I was working), it was a very humbling and bittersweet season to live life again as a student. There were many times I just wanted to pack my bags and head home, but fortunately I persisted! This was the opportunity for me to re-think what it is that I wanted in life, to understand that my identity is not tied to what I do or how much I earn, but who I am. I was grateful for that season because I learnt life lessons that helped to set me free, free to be me!

I learnt through this experience that sometimes a setback can be a form of set up! This is if we choose to respond positively towards it and learn from it.

During that season, I walked to school and noticed along the way a little agapanthus flower bud. It was very small.

Slowly, I saw little flower heads burst out of the bud. In due season, it bloomed into a glorious flower – in all its beauty, even to nourish others around it.

How did that big bunch of flowers manage to hide in that small bud?

That was when I was reminded of the ancient verse:

"Do not despise the day of small beginnings."
Book of Zechariah (520 BCE)

In due season, if we were to feed the seed that is in us consistently, it will bloom into something beautiful, bigger than we can ever imagine.

Do you have a seed, a dream that is in your heart that you hope to achieve? Do you believe there is more for you? I want to encourage you there is. And the good news is, the seed is ALREADY in you.

Fast forward ten years, I have achieved my MBA with the Dean's award and started my own consultancy firm. I am now a Gallup Certified Strengths Coach, an author and speaker. I finally got to transition from corporate to what I love doing, helping others find their unique voice and excel in life. Looking back, I'm thankful for this bittersweet season, for it gave me the grace and opportunity to ask myself some hard questions, to understand who I really am and what I really want.

CLARITY is the future of authority.

I want to encourage you that there is a better you that you can step into. You can realise the dreams that are in you! Never ever despise your days of small beginnings. Just like Sun Tzu, by using strategies, he managed to defeat a city that had ten times his resources. Likewise, we can achieve great things regardless of what we have, or where we start. We just have to understand the strategies we can apply towards our goal. I have broken the strategies into a simple formula called *Staircase to Authority*.

I ask you to walk with me and find clarity as you read this book and step up the Staircase to Authority. Let clarity be the power that propels you upwards into your personal authority.

Keep on investing in yourself and I am sure you'll soon see the best version of you. One day, you will look back, give out a big sigh, and smile. You will be grateful you chose to believe in yourself. You will be grateful you have watered that seed that is in you, for it has grown into a glorious tree that bears fruit that nourishes many others around you. You will feel fulfilled and satisfied as you stand amazed by the greatness you have achieved.

Clarity is POWER and you can unleash that power.

You matter.

I believe in you.

Love,
Ruth Saw

Chapter 1

CLARITY IS POWER

UNDERSTANDING THE IMPORTANCE OF CLARITY

CLARITY INCREASES OUR VALUE

———

"LIKE A DIAMOND,
THE MORE CLARITY
WE HAVE, THE MORE
VALUE WE BRING."

Ruth Saw

THE WORD CLARITY MEANS THE QUALITY OF BEING CLEAR and easy to understand; the ability to see, hear, and think clearly and not be confused. Another definition describes it as clearness of thought or style. Clarity describes what you see, hear, or even do.

If you see spring water coming from the mountains, you see clarity. Clarity is refreshing. If you hear a lovely voice, that's voice clarity. Clarity touches hearts. If you bring clarity to a situation, that's intelligence. Clarity solves problems. Clarity affects every area of our lives. Clarity is often also described as perception or understanding. For personal clarity, it is the perception or understanding of who we really are and what our next steps are.

If you look at the etymology or the root word of clarity, it is clarté. Clarté means brightness, radiance, glory and splendour.

You know those times in your life when you have a bounce in your step, when there is a sense of clearness that comes from within, when there is a radiance coming from you, when there is a glorious splendour about you, that is when you have solid clarity of who you are! Clarity is power, for it is where we all shine bright, with radiance, glory, and splendour. That is the journey clarity can bring.

Okay, so practically speaking, what does this mean? I reviewed a number of different speakers and influencers and found that while these influencers are very different, all spoke with authority. They have a magnetic way of influencing, effecting change, and winning people over. What is the common thread among them? What makes their voice, their message, so unique and how do they speak with such authority?

Martin Luther King Jr. was most well-known for his speech "I have a dream." He was an American Christian minister, activist and leader in the Civil Rights Movement from 1955. Years later, even now, people still resonate with his speech. He sparked off a movement that continued beyond his time.

Mother Teresa founded the Missionaries of Charity in 1950, that had over 4,500 nuns and was active in 133 countries in 2012. She fed the poor and hugged the dying. She also stood with various Presidents of the United States and won numerous awards, one of which was the Nobel Peace Prize in 1979. She started this glorious journey by simply packing her bags to go to India, and feeding one child at a time.

I've also looked at other influencers; they are all very different. For example, Mother Teresa is extremely different from Martin Luther King Jr.! Although they spoke with different voices, they seem to have the same formula. They all spoke from a place of passion and purpose. As I read their stories, I noticed that their purpose and greatness unfolded as they followed their heart, a step at a time. There is absolute clarity in their otherwise unique personalities when they speak or lead. This is why I believe these influencers could make such a big difference in the world – simply because they knew who they were, and they took that first step. They also spoke from their purpose, finding the energy and stamina to continue on their chosen road, and doors just opened into something bigger than they could ask, think, or imagine. This is indeed the path of least resistance! That's authority.

Here's a personal example of someone who influenced me. When I came to Australia, all I wanted was to complete my MBA and settle in Australia. The first few years were tough; I was trying to survive; I had no purpose nor passion. All I knew was to do the best I could in my studies and look for a job for financial stability. Fortunately, I personally went to a church that brought in excellent speakers, and they inspired and motivated me. My pastor influenced me to see retirement differently because he was fulfilling his purpose and didn't want to stop at 60. That's when I asked myself, "What does retirement look like to me? What is my purpose and passion?" That sparked my obsession to find my personal clarity. I took a long time discovering myself, which is why I'm writing this book, to share with others what I discovered works. Hopefully, it will save you from a few hard knocks!

Indra Nooyi, the former CEO of PepsiCo and the first Asian female global CEO in the United States of America, named as Fortune's second most powerful woman in business in 2017, said this:

> "An important attribute of success is to be
> yourself. Never hide what makes you, you."

What about you? Have you been comparing yourself with others and feeling that you've fallen short? Do you have clarity about who you are, and do you know how you can maximise this?

There is a common myth that we find clarity when we grow older: just go with the flow and things will unfold. Is this true? It is both yes and no. I realised that I must have the intention to find clarity and take steps towards it, before I learn to go with the flow wisely, to see how life unfolds. Otherwise, I'm just drifting, living my life meeting others' expectations without thinking what my personal heart desires are.

Ralph Waldo Emerson, American lecturer, philosopher and poet said:

> *"To be yourself in a world that is constantly*
> *trying to make you something else is*
> *the greatest accomplishment."*

There are often people who are middle-aged that talk about a time of midlife crisis. It can be caused by a combination of changes in career and relationships or aging, and possible regrets in different areas in their lives, be it career, relationships, family or personal health.

Very often, these individuals are searching for an undefined dream or goal. Or perhaps they may fear humiliation among more successful colleagues.

At the root of all these issues is a sense that perhaps there is something missing. There is often a tragic wisdom in such mid-life crises, as these individuals come to a realisation of the emptiness of much of what they used to strive for (even if what they replace it with is not always particularly wise). It is as if they reach the top of the ladder of success only to find that it was leaning on the wrong wall.

There are many studies out there that link depression, health problems, anxiety and regrets to unmet needs. I think at the core of these issues, these unmet needs, is the lack of clarity of who we are and what we really need.

Companies nowadays are investing a lot in having their employees complete personality assessments in order to find out who they are and maximise their strengths. A Gallup analysis reveals that people who use their strengths every day are three times more likely to report having an excellent quality of life, six times more likely to be engaged at work, 8% more productive and 15% less likely to quit their jobs. Companies are also investing a lot in the communication of their vision, mission, and values. They know that employees flourish when they understand how they fit into the company's vision.

> Ask yourself, as the CEO of your own life, how much are you investing in yourself?

These companies invest a lot in strengths-based training, and I'm sure they do it because there is a tangible return on investment (ROI) – better performance and profits.

What about you?

Ask yourself, as the CEO of your own life, how much are you investing in yourself? Are you investing in your personal clarity to get a better performance and to be more engaged in your own life?

For example, if I'm the CEO of Ruth Saw Inc., what can I do to maximise the efficiency, the quality of life, and the returns of Ruth Saw Inc.? How much do you believe in your potential? Could there be more? Thomas Edison said, "If we did all the things we are capable of doing, we would literally astonish ourselves." If you could see yourself as you could be, you would look better than you ever imagined!

People who believe in themselves get better jobs and perform better in them than those who don't. Martin Seligman, self-help author, did some research at a major life insurance company and found that sales people who expected to succeed sold 37% more insurance than those who didn't. Even the bible declares, "As a man thinks, so is he." (Proverbs 23:7) The question is, how can you believe when you cannot see what's possible? Clarity is the key to unlock your potential.

So first and foremost, congratulations on reading this book! I want to acknowledge you for taking time to invest in yourself, to invest in your clarity.

It is okay to take time to discover yourself, to find out who you are and what you want. Don't ever feel stuck; you can do something about it! Once you achieve that, half the battle is won. Then, you just need to work out concrete steps towards your goal, and based on your understanding of yourself, find a way that motivates and excites you. I call this the path of least resistance. Clarity provides greater action and persistence in our lives. When we realise we are only leading half a life, the other half will haunt us until we take action and develop it.

> Clarity is the key to unlock your potential.

To find out who you are, it is important to look at your talents and gifts, to understand what energises you, because that is where you'll find success. It will help you in every area of your life, even in making decisions.

Let me illustrate with money, an example most people can understand. Imagine you have been clear that you want to pay off your mortgage as soon as possible. When you happen to see a beautiful but very expensive couch for sale, would you buy it? The answer is simple! NO. You have made a commitment to pay off debt; making that decision takes just a split second.

> Clarity provides greater action and persistence in our lives.

Far too often, we waste a lot of time considering too many options, thinking we are doing our due diligence in our decisions, only to find that the root of the issue is that we have no clarity. I dare say, the first due diligence we need is to find our personal clarity!

Finding clarity gives us ease, in all that we do, even in decisions. It helps us save time, be efficient, and be happy with our decisions.

Look at a diamond. What determines its value? The greater the clarity, the more value it has. The prices of diamonds with different clarity grades can double every few grades. True flawless diamonds are very rare.

Fortunately for us humans, we can find greater clarity. When we have greater clarity, we communicate more effectively to ourselves in decision making, and also to others. Having clarity not only benefits us, it also benefits others around us. Like a diamond, the more clarity we have, the more value we bring. The more clarity we have, the more we will shine.

WHY DO WE NEED CLARITY?

HAVING CLARITY BENEFITS US

You may have heard the famous quote: "Love your neighbour as yourself." A lot of kind-hearted people focus on loving their neighbour, which I think is great and we need more compassionate people out there. My question is: "To what extent do you love yourself, since we are to love our neighbour AS ourselves?"

The more we can accept and love ourselves, the more we can accept and love others. Self-love is a big topic and I will not attempt to discuss it here at length. However, if we want to step into our authority with confidence, it starts with being comfortable in our own skin.

> Like a diamond, the more clarity we have, the more value we bring.

How do you do that when you don't love yourself? How do we love ourselves when we don't know who we are? Are we beating ourselves up unnecessarily by comparing ourselves to others who may be very differently wired from us?

When we are clear about who we are, we will know when to say no, and when to say yes. Have you wasted unnecessary time considering all options simply by not knowing what you want?

When we know who we are, we will know how to approach our tasks so that our strengths and talents will support us and energise us in reaching the goal. Isn't that just freedom from within? Someone shared with me that for us to reach higher, we must dig deeper. How liberating that can be!

Louise Lynn Hay was an American motivational author and the founder of Hay House. She authored several self-help books and she said:

> "To me, to be enlightened is to go within and to know who and what we really are, and to know that we have the ability to change for the better by loving and taking care of ourselves. It's not selfish to love ourselves. It clears us so that we can love ourselves enough to love other people."

HAVING CLARITY BENEFITS OUR RELATIONSHIPS

For our friends, when we communicate clearly what we want, we avoid misunderstandings. Have you been in a group trying to look for a place to eat? Then everyone says, "I'm flexible. It depends on where you want to go." What happens next? Everyone is so flexible they just hang around the same spot without making any decisions. Or perhaps they will then consider all options in a big group and spend time on mindless conversations and walking around looking at different places to go.

Finally, when someone says, "Hey, there's a Japanese place here. I feel like Japanese. Shall we do that?" Then the whole group starts moving because they have a direction. This is a simple example. However, situations like this take place a lot in personal life and at work.

Very often our friends and family want to help us, but they don't know how until we articulate it. That's where we can build the relationship by voicing what we want and supporting one another. It begins with clarity.

Having clarity can also help us be aware of our blind spots, avoid frustrations, and protect our relationships. I'll share about this in more detail in Chapter 4. A blind spot is an area in our lives that we do not notice. If we are not mindful of it or don't take care of it, we may end up with negative consequences. If you drive, you know what overlooking a blind spot can do! For example, I am wired to always think about the future. I get energised thinking about my long-term visions, but very often I forget to enjoy the present, especially time with my friends. This can cause strain in my friendships. That is my blind spot. I have to be aware of it and schedule time to think about the future on my own, so that I can choose to be present when I am with my friends.

> For us to reach higher, we must dig deeper.

You may have heard of the book *The Five Love Languages: How to Express Heartfelt Commitment to Your Mate* by Gary Chapman. It outlines five ways to express and experience love between romantic partners that Chapman calls love languages, and how important it is for one to express love in the way the partner desires. I believe the book has saved quite a lot of relationships since it was released in 1992! Understanding who our loved ones are helps us to express love to them the way they desire, and it strengthens our relationships.

Having clarity also helps us set healthy boundaries that can protect our relationships. I have heard of so many cases where students choose their course of study because their parents want it. They can cope with it, but they don't like it and they become frustrated or resentful.

If you were to look at the frustrations that you have felt in relationships, have you stopped to reflect on what the root cause could be? Perhaps you are in a business role that manages people. What are the common frustrations you have felt? Remember, your subordinates are very different from you. If it happens with more than one person, the common denominator is you! Could it be possible that perhaps it was your blind spot, or was it an issue of clarity or boundaries?

HAVING CLARITY BENEFITS OUR BUSINESS OR PROFESSION

In this current age, we have too much information. It's not about the content you can give; it's how clearly you can communicate, and whether they trust you. In a crowded market, the more clarity you have, the more you'll stand out. The more authentic you are, the more people are able to trust you.

It's about how you can be specific and clear in your message to attract your right clients. It's how you can break it down into very simple bite-sized chunks so that your customers, without a doubt, can understand, implement and find value. When you have clarity, you'll be so clear in your message that you'll attract people that will need your service and are willing to pay for it.

All companies that are strong in branding and marketing know this. They are clear in their message and their targeted market (which we will discuss in Chapter 5). When we read "Just do it," we think of Nike. When we hear "I have a dream," we think of Martin Luther King Jr. Imagine your customers remembering your company or you this way!

Or perhaps you are in a corporate role. Do you know who you need to work with to complement your strengths and values? Do you understand your team members well enough to know what will motivate them? Imagine you are able to clearly articulate what you are looking for during your performance review, what difference would that make?

Someone I knew was given a promotion to management, but this person knew he would rather be an individual contributor as a salesperson. He knew he was driven by meeting new people and he loved the flexibility of time as he had a young child. He said no to the promotion, and he said yes to his son, even though the title was good, and it was an opportunity to a management role. He was clear about what he wanted at that point of time in his life. His main value was family and he managed to have a strong bond with his son. Years later, when his son was older and he found a partner to support the family, he finally said yes to the management role. He brought his family values to the company, treated his staff like his family and was a great senior executive. Do you know what are your values and your priorities?

If you are running a business, having clarity can have a direct impact on your bottom-line. As a procurement professional for the last two decades, my main role was to create savings for the company based on what they currently spend. I worked as a consultant for companies who wanted to reduce their costs, and I had to quickly produce results so that they would continue to engage me. What I would do first, instead of looking at what needed to be done operationally, was to take a step back, and to understand what they were spending on. Then I'd break these into categories (or buckets) to identify where I should focus and provide a roadmap of activities we could do to save money.

Then, by using the Pareto principle (focusing on the top 20% of suppliers that contribute to the 80% of the spend), I would work through which projects I should start first, to get the most savings the quickest way.

Once we were told to reduce spend for logistics for a monopoly supplier, which I initially thought was impossible. In this instance, it was the only airline that flew into this country. The supplier could charge whatever he wanted, and my client had to pay because he needed the service. The spend was over tens of millions and no one had managed to reduce it for the last three years. The client then engaged us to look at ways to lower cost. We had to think out of the box. While others were focusing on building relationships, negotiating with the supplier who simply refused to budge, we decided to review and find clarity on the actual service requirements. We figured that every flight was never full! With a few adjustments, we reduced the flights to two times a week instead of three and saved the company over ten million dollars! What my client couldn't achieve in the first three years of using this supplier, we managed to deliver in just a few months. That is the power of clarity!

For me to be able to save money as a procurement professional, I need to find absolute clarity on the buyer's requirements, as well as the supplier's competitive landscape. This allows me to negotiate a good deal and create a win-win situation for both parties. These are the same questions that can be applied to every area of our life: personal, relationships or even corporate. What do we need? What do we want? What do suppliers/others need? What do suppliers/others want? This was always my secret sauce to reduce spend for every company I have worked for. I am proud to say that I have always reduced costs, even if the market was not in favour of us! I accomplished that by using the same few questions, by tapping on clarity.

This is why I absolutely LOVE Sun Tzu's quote at the start of this book: "Know yourself, know your opponent, a hundred battles, a hundred victories." My secret sauce is based on a tried and tested strategy way back in 500 BCE! Best of all, this strategy can be applied in all situations!

This quote will be the foundation of the Staircase of Authority, and it will be elaborated on in Chapter 3.

WHAT ARE THE CONSEQUENCES OF NOT HAVING CLARITY?

There are seven consequences of not having clarity, I certainly hope we don't learn it the hard way. By having clarity, we can avoid most of these issues. They are as follows and some will be elaborated on in the following chapters.

1. Our blind spots can hinder us.
2. We waste unnecessary time and effort.
3. We carry unnecessary labels about ourselves.
4. We are left with fewer choices as time goes on.
5. It can become hard to receive help.
6. We don't know when to say no.
7. We don't say yes to opportunities.

I hope this chapter has demonstrated that clarity is of the utmost importance. It affects us, our relationships, and even our business or career. You may feel it is counter-intuitive to take a step back and find clarity, as most of us just want to get things done and get so busy that we can't find time to take a step back. It feels uncomfortable to take a step back. However, we can't afford not to.

I use the analogy of an arrow. For it to plunge forward quickly and effectively, it needs to be pulled back. Finding clarity sometimes feels like being pulled back. What you need to know is: to the extent it is pulled back, to that extent it can propel forward.

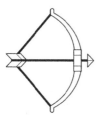

"Just like shooting an arrow, we pull back to find clarity so that we can propel forward with speed."

Finding clarity can sometimes feel uncomfortable as we may have to ask ourselves some hard questions. Or perhaps, we are in transition and we feel very uncomfortable, like we are on shaky ground. Sometimes, it feels easier to go back to what we are familiar with. Just like the example of the arrow above, the arrow needs to stay in the bow when it is pulled back before it can propel forward.

Fortunately, it is not difficult to find clarity. I have provided very simple steps to find clarity. However, it requires you to be intentional. Clarity NEVER comes when we drift.

The following chapters will unpack how we can find clarity and step into our personal authority with strength and confidence.

Chapter 2

THE 3W
FRAMEWORK

3 SIMPLE KEYS TO UNLOCKING CLARITY

CLARITY UNLOCKS OUR PATH

———

"THE HOW TO SUCCESS DEPENDS ON WHO YOU ARE."

Ruth Saw

———————————

CLARITY IS NOT LIKE A MYSTERY BOX THAT WE CAN'T UNLOCK. However, to find clarity, we need to be intentional about it. Clarity doesn't just turn up.

Be intentional and row your boat towards your destination. Sometimes it may not be a straight path; sometimes we have to wait; at times, there are obstacles we need to navigate around, but as long as we continually paddle and check our direction, all will be well. Be open and willing to enter a season of uncertainty as you are exploring. Trust the process. Sometimes we may have doubts; it is normal in times of uncertainty and that's okay. Face your doubts and watch them crumble away as you take action to grow. The waiting time is nothing, compared to the years you have lived! Also be willing to take on the daily grind for practical reasons.

Choose to believe you have a purpose and watch things unfold. Sometimes we need to see it in our hearts and minds before things come to pass. The only person that needs to see the greatness in you is you.

Would you please give yourself permission to explore, to even sometimes be wrong and to learn about yourself?

Below shows the 3W framework to finding clarity.

THE 3W FRAMEWORK

1 — CLARITY COMES FROM WITHIN

We need to understand who we are and what our talents are. One of the easiest ways to find out what our talents are is through a Gallup Clifton StrengthsFinder Assessment. The assessment has been used by over 20 million people and backed up with over six decades of research. It is a personality assessment that reveals what our top 5 talents are. It helps provide the language and vocabulary to describe our talents, and how we are uniquely wired. It also provides possible areas that could be our blind spots.

Talents simply represent the way we think, feel, or behave naturally. These talents, after much investment become our strengths. In short, talents are potential, strengths are performance. It is a philosophy of focusing on what we are good at, and getting better, rather than focusing on our weaknesses. We call people who do that strength-based people.

According to the Clifton StrengthsFinder assessment from Gallup, the chances of us having the exact same strengths in the same order is **1 in 33 million!** We are unique. The treasure is in you; you just have to unlock it.

Have you felt that you have a dream and vision, and as you share with others, you get conflicting responses to the point you get confused and frustrated? This is because we are all uniquely wired with differing perspectives. Soliciting feedback without asking ourselves what we want can leave us more confused. Be careful whom you seek advice from. A better way to find clarity is to ask within, to understand our strengths and desires, and to learn to follow our heart. Of course, we still need to seek wise counsel from mentors and coaches to help accelerate our growth.

Growing up in a traditional Asian family, I have been conditioned to meet the expectations of others. So, I found understanding what I want and who I am, a very difficult task. I had to learn to increase the volume of my heart's desires and drown the volume of the demands around me. I had to learn to lead myself with my heart, instead of only thinking rationally about what others want. It's a daily decision that has now become a habit.

Stop looking outside but look within. Ask yourself: "What are your strengths, talents, and skills that makes you, you?"

Life can sometimes be a reflection of our clarity. If it is blur and if we cannot articulate it effectively for friends and family to support us, we lose the opportunity for accelerated growth through the help they can provide. Most people around us want us to succeed and they genuinely want to help us. However, when we are unclear and unable to articulate it, it's hard for them to help or support us.

> Clarity comes from WITHIN.

I have seen parents who have the resources to send their children to any school of their choice, in any part of the world. It depends on whether the child knows what he wants. I have seen children who knew what they wanted and were given the opportunity to study in the best schools. They turned out to be excellent in what they do.

I have also seen children who dabbled with one school after another, one course after another, and they are still studying and relying on their parents. The difference is the former knew what they wanted, but the latter didn't.

The very first key to finding clarity is that clarity comes from within. It's about understanding our strengths and talents, how we are wired, so that we can create strategies that work for us.

So how do you find clarity from within?

Clarity in the dictionary literally means clearness. It means easy to see, to hear, and to understand.

In very simple terms, these are the 3 simple steps to finding clarity within.

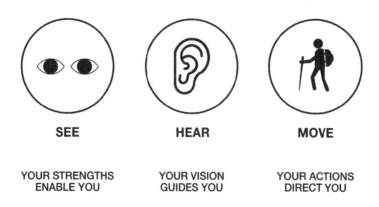

SEE	HEAR	MOVE
YOUR STRENGTHS ENABLE YOU	YOUR VISION GUIDES YOU	YOUR ACTIONS DIRECT YOU

A. SEE

The very first step to finding clarity from within is to SEE. This sounds simple, but it may not be easy. It's like holding a mirror to your face, as you have to face yourself, blemishes and all! It is the ability to see past our blemishes and find our beauty! This is exactly what we coaches do. We hold a mirror to your face. Sometimes, we address blind spots that you need to be aware of, and then we work together to find out how we can overcome them. You can't change what you are not willing to confront. We need to improve our sight before we work on our strategy.

Have you been to a hotel where they have a vanity mirror in the bathroom that has a mirror on both sides? One side is a normal mirror, the other side is a magnifying mirror. When I first looked at the magnifying mirror, I got a shock! All my blemishes, pores and wrinkles were enlarged! Sometimes we want to look away; my encouragement is to stay. Stay till we can look at ourselves, blemishes and all, and actually love what we see. That takes effort. That's the journey of clarity that I hope to prepare you for. When you don't feel like facing yourself, stay till you see the beauty that you bring.

Perhaps there are things we need to correct, such as our blind spots. We can address them first by being aware and by nurturing ourselves, not by beating ourselves up! Clarity is not about pinpointing all your weaknesses; it is a change of perspective. It is to look into the mirror to see our beauty.

All of us are uniquely wired for greatness, and it takes clarity to see who we can become.

LET YOUR STRENGTHS ENABLE YOU

Do you realise that WHO and HOW have the same letters, just in a different order? A lot of people focus on the HOW; however, it is not effective until you know WHO you are. The HOW to success depends on WHO you are.

Let me give you a very simple example that I believe everyone can relate to. I have a friend who has been trying to lose weight for years but in vain.

What do you think he should do to lose weight? Most would say get a personal trainer and keep a strict diet. But it just didn't work for him! He didn't enjoy the process. His weight went on a yo-yo pattern; he would lose some weight and gain it back again.

He realised that he didn't enjoy the personal trainer session, as he did not like being pushed. He also had a lot of friends who loved going to the pub after work, so it became difficult for him to follow a strict diet, because he preferred to join his community and he didn't want to be different.

Based on the strengths he discovered through the Gallup Clifton StrengthsFinder report, this friend realised that he loved to seek consensus with others, and he also

> The HOW to success depends on WHO you are.

loved community. Being motivated by peace and harmony, he tended to avoid conflict with others. The personal training to him felt like a conflict! That was his blind spot.

Understanding how he was wired, he asked himself, "How can I use my personality to support me in my weight loss goal?" We decided perhaps he could join classes instead of personal trainer sessions. Because the class was so energetic, he kept up in pace to be in harmony with the group. He also found a community at the gym classes who enjoyed healthy food and started hanging out with them. Changing his diet suddenly became a breeze because everyone around him was eating healthy. It wasn't difficult like before when he was trying to diet on his own. He lost 10 kilograms in a couple of months.

What he could not do in years, he managed to achieve in months by understanding who he was and applying the right strategies.

My encouragement to you is that there is no one specific way to do a task. It's great to seek advice, but in the end, find a way that works best for you – based on who you are.

Read how-to books based on the understanding of who you are and adapt accordingly. For example, if the book says wake up and do xyz early but you know you are most alert at night, there is no shame in doing what the book says at night, your most productive time.

You could save a lot of time and enjoy the process a lot more by having more clarity on WHO you are!

Would you please take time to look at your talents and believe you were uniquely designed to become someone great, just the way you are? Don't worry about the HOW; that can be discussed and worked out.

The first step is to SEE: see your beauty and let your STRENGTHS enable you.

B. HEAR

Oprah Winfrey says "Follow your instincts. That's where true wisdom manifests itself." In other words, wisdom comes from within. So the second step is to hear our heart. Do you notice the word hear lies in the word heart? This means that if we do not hear, we do not have a heart!

It is the heart that keeps us alive. Hear it, listen to your heart! Do you take time to hear what's in your heart?

Carl Jung, a Swiss psychiatrist said:

*"Your vision will become clear only when
you can look into your own heart. Who looks
outside, dreams; who looks inside, awakes."*

What about the word gut? In English, we say things like, I feel in my gut to do this. Very often, it is used interchangeably from feeling in your gut to listening to your heart. Interestingly, the same word guts is used for courage! My question to you is this, "Do you have the guts to follow your heart?" It takes courage to follow your heart!

Remember there is a lot of research linking anxiety and depression to unmet needs. I personally believe these are the unmet needs of your heart. When was the last time you paused and listened to your heart?

I have been blessed to work with many clients to help expound on their strengths and talents to find clarity. However, there have been a lot of clients who did not want to listen to their hearts. They want me to tell them what to do based the personality tests. I cannot, for I am not them.

What I can offer is that based on their heart desires, their values, their strengths and gifts, we can then discuss how they can use their unique personalities to maximise their potential. I work with them to uncover strategies to get to where they want to be, but I cannot choose their goals for them.

As a coach, my role is to ask the right questions, but you are responsible to answer them and dig deep. Again, one of my favourite lines is: "To reach higher, you need to dig deeper."

It is in you. For some, it takes a longer time to "tune in" and uncover it, but it can be done. It starts with the intention and belief that you have the right to fulfil your heart's desires.

Very often, we analyse till we are paralysed and become stuck. That's because we left the heart out of the equation! I firmly believe that our vision is not a matter of intellect but a matter of hearing our hearts. A vision from your heart energises you.

> Our vision is not a matter of intellect but a matter of hearing our hearts.

Give yourself the permission and the right to be happy. Sometimes it is perceived as humility to put yourself down and put everyone else's needs before you. This is the biggest lie ever! You matter. Hear your heart. When you follow your heart, you'll find the greatest satisfaction. You deserve to be happy. Interestingly, when you are happy, people around you will celebrate with you.

HOW TO HEAR YOUR HEART

Do you know that in ancient Hebrew, the word heart means inner man, heart, mind, and will? If that is true, it means that our hearts and minds should connect, or are one and the same. But very often, we catch ourselves in situations where our heart wants to go in a direction, while our mind tells us otherwise.

While I believe it is important to strategise and think though our decision, I find that our minds often rationalise ourselves out, due to fear or limiting beliefs. One simple way to hear our hearts is to journal very quickly, not giving our minds time to overthink.

Keep on journaling and you'll find a pattern. The voice of your heart will shout louder, and it will become clearer.

The second step to finding clarity within is to HEAR: hear your heart, let your VISION guide you.

C. MOVE

William Jennings Bryan was an American orator and politician from Nebraska. He mentioned that understanding our talents alone is not enough. It is the key choices we make that will set us apart from others who have talents alone. He said, "Destiny is not a matter of chance, it is a matter of choice; it is not a thing to be waited for, it is a thing to be achieved."

The final step is to move. We need to take action to understand ourselves better. We need to decide quickly, move and then recalibrate; this will help us evaluate our decisions. I find that a lot of us are waiting for clarity to come. But logically speaking, if we notice something far away and it looks blur, what do we do? We walk forward so that the picture becomes clearer. It is the same with finding clarity. We need to move forward to have greater clarity.

> Your vision is proven perfect by your movement, not decision.

Have you been to an optometrist? This person tests your eyesight and puts on multiple lenses for you to wear.

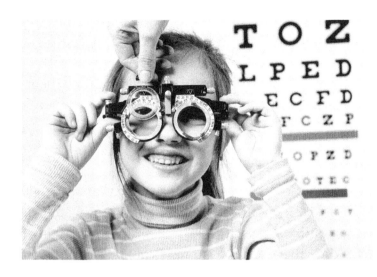

He will test each lens and start asking questions, "Is this lens clearer or the other?"

Who decides?

You do. You must reply. You can't say, "I don't know". Your clarity is your responsibility. Sometimes, both lenses are similar, then it is really up to your choice which one you pick. Once you have decided, you wear the lenses and go out in life; if it didn't fit, you can easily go back to the optometrist to arrange for another lens. The purpose of having perfect vision is so that we can live our lives with ease. Your vision is proven perfect by your movement, not decision.

Likewise, in your personal life, take the first step to try different things that excite you till you find one that suits you. What is the worst that can happen? At least you've learnt what you like and don't like. As you try, you are allowing and building your heart's voice so that you can hear it louder. I see so many clients who don't know what they want, but they certainly know what they don't want! By testing and trying, we are just going through the elimination process to find what works.

I think that is the same with life. Sometimes life presents you different paths that could work for you. It is up to you to choose what you are comfortable with. The worst thing to do is not even take a step. Both opportunities presented to you then just remain as dreams or potential, not reality. Explore yourself as you explore growth. Taking the first step can be uncomfortable, because stretching and growing is always uncomfortable. But as you continue, you'll pick up momentum and you'll realise, it's actually quite fun. Because you get to design your own clarity!

Live the life you were meant to. See yourself as you could be and then do everything in your power to believe you can become that person. That is critical to your success.

I want to add that, if you are reading this book, it means you have a desire to be the best version of yourself. Let me give you permission to dream and believe what's possible for you. Empower yourself to take the first step.

The third step to finding clarity within is to MOVE: let your ACTIONS direct you.

2 — CLARITY COMES AS YOU WALK

Because action is so important, I'm re-emphasizing it as the second key to finding clarity. Clarity unfolds as you WALK into it. I used to think I could start moving towards my dreams only after I had absolute clarity on what I want. I have found that this itself has paralysed me many times towards what I want to achieve. I realised clarity is a journey; as we take a step forward, the road ahead unfolds more.

Life is not stationary nor static. It's not a picture but a movie. You are the director of this movie. What do film directors say to start creating the movie? Take Action! Likewise, if you feel you have an idea about what you want but hope to have more clarity or you are still deciding between choices, it is okay. Just take action, take the first step and see how you go.

Keep on going. If you have started with an intention, if you have learnt to listen to your heart, then the rest is a journey. Have you wondered how whales migrate or how turtles return to the site where they were born? How do birds migrate to the north, knowing where to go?

I don't believe they knew the location right at the start. According to research, they can identify the place based on their ability to understand the magnetic fields. As they move in a general direction, they get to read the magnetic fields and re-adjust accordingly to find the exact spot.

Likewise, if we are able to follow our hearts' desires from within and to keep on going, we will get there. Clarity is a journey; it becomes clearer as we walk along, as long as we know our overall direction.

Bruce Lee is known professionally as a Hong Kong-American actor, director, martial artist, martial arts instructor and philosopher. He left Hong Kong at the age of 18 and went to the United States where he enrolled in the University of Washington and pursued a degree in philosophy. Do you think he knew he wanted to be an actor before he went to school? I don't think so! He followed his passion and doors opened up. Clarity is an action. Take the first step and keep on going and watch how life unfolds.

Bruce Lee himself said:

> *"Knowing is not enough, we must apply.*
> *Willing is not enough, we must do."*

Keep on walking; otherwise, you may feel stuck. Have you tried crossing a stream on rocks or crossing a mountain on a bridge? The fastest way to reach the other side is to keep walking!

If you remain stuck on one rock or on the bridge, life can look scary and feel terribly uncomfortable, while trying so hard to balance there for a long time. Taking a step back is actually harder as your eyes are looking ahead, so you might as well move forward!

Clarity is a journey. Once you have uncovered your vision, move and you'll find clarity!

I have so many people who say, "Oh, I'm waiting for more clarity before I proceed." My question is: "If you have been living all these years without clarity, would clarity come if you wait longer?" One of my favourite quotes is the quote often attributed to Albert Einstein:

"The definition of insanity is doing the same thing over and over and expecting a different result."

Has what you were thinking before served you? If not, why not give it a shot and believe that you are uniquely designed on this earth for a reason? And keep on walking it out till you feel that your destiny has become your skin, till you shine from within.

I know that there are a lot of teachings out there that say you've got to find your purpose before you do anything. I am here to challenge that. I feel that your purpose unfolds as you move forward, as long as you always hear your heart.

As a Christian, there are some principles in the bible that I find easy to understand. I have often used them to counsel others who are seeking clarity. Please allow me to share the same analogy, as it is easy to understand.

> Your purpose unfolds as you move forward, as long as you always hear your heart.

Some people hope and pray and keep on waiting for God to show them their path before they make any step. Maybe they were hoping for God to appear in front of them and tell them what to do. I would remind them that God has given us a brain and heart to discern and decide! We are empowered with the ability to make choices.

God also says He is a lamp to our feet, so the path gets clearer as you step forward. He never said He was a torch on our heads! Whether you believe in God or not, trust God or trust your heart enough to embark on the journey and watch your purpose unfold as you step forward. Your heart will speak and provide you feedback as you tune into your heart.

If we keep on halting, we may end up just having potential but never actually step into it! Les Brown is an American motivational speaker, author, former radio DJ and former television host. He said this beautifully; this quote reminds me to continually walk into my destiny:

> "The graveyard is the richest place on earth, because it is here that you will find all the hopes and dreams that were never fulfilled, the books that were never written, the songs that were never sung, the inventions that were never shared, the cures that were never discovered, all because someone was too afraid to take that first step, keep with the problem, or determined to carry out their dream."

Others resign to fate; when they meet an obstacle, they decide maybe it's not meant to be. Then they look for the next thing that comes along. That is drifting. Don't get me wrong. I believe it is important to be open to life and what it brings but it can be very tiring being swayed from one area to another.

Action leads to direction. Just look at nature and learn from it. When there is fresh flowing water, everything lives. Stagnant water breeds flies and bacteria. It becomes toxic and unsafe to drink. What type of water would you rather be? Move and be that fresh, flowing water that brings life. At least when you are exploring, you can still bring life to others around you! Confidence shows up when we show up. Keep on going.

I love to bushwalk in the Australian countryside. We get the map and plot out where to go. However, sometimes, because of weather or other reasons, we might have to take alternative routes when we reach a certain place and see what's ahead. All this happens after we take the first step. There's only so much we can prepare by looking at the map, but we still need to walk in it and recalibrate many times.

Action leads to direction.

When I first started bushwalking, I was overwhelmed by the distance, but the leader said something very wise. He said, "All you need to do is to put your foot in front of the other. Just repeat 40,000 times!" Clarity comes as you take each step. You become more ready when you start walking. Opportunities open when you are ready.

3 — CLARITY COMES BASED ON THE WORDS YOU SAY AND THE WORDS YOU CHOOSE TO LISTEN TO

We understand clarity is a journey, and we need to walk into it. However, how fast or slow the journey is, depends greatly on the third key to clarity. It is the WORDS we say and the WORDS we choose to listen to. It depends on the friends you mix with: are they empowering you, or are they dragging you down? Perhaps, it could be a negative word or label that was spoken to you when you were very young, and you accepted it. Never give away the power of your potential to someone's negative voice!

Imagine different words stored in your brain: positive words relating to a healthy brain, and negative words clouding your brain. It's hard to think clearly if most parts of your brain are cloudy. However, if you are conscious of what you choose to accept and you intentionally make it a habit to filter only empowering thoughts, then, it is actually easier to find clarity.

Coming from an Asian family, my mum used to scold me and call me stupid. She told me she should have left me at the rubbish dump. For a while, I believed I was unwanted and a burden and ended up doing very badly in school. I was also often sick.

Fortunately, I met someone in my teenage years who told me I had potential and believed in me. I had to constantly learn to disassociate with that label of stupid and rise up to my potential. I managed to graduate from my MBA with the Dean's Medal Award. I'm not writing this to brag, but to

> Never give away the power of your potential to someone's negative voice!

share the seriousness of how words can change our lives and our destinies. Who are you listening to? What words are you accepting in your life?

Do you know our words have creative power? Great leaders change nations with their words. If you want to change your life, change the way you talk to yourself too. When you change your words, you change your destiny. You absolutely own the narrative of your life.

What you articulate determines your belief. Your belief in who you are can lift you and empower you. Your friend's belief in you will also fuel your growth. How do you know your friend believes in you? By the words they say! Hence, the words you speak and the words you receive are very important and pivotal to your success.

> When you change your words, you change your destiny.

What are the words you choose to speak over your life? Are they empowering you to move further, step higher?

Make the effort to ensure your friends are positive and supportive. Of course, you still need to have mentors and coaches whom you trust to tell you things that you need to hear, not just what you want to hear. Be very careful whom you solicit feedback from. Get feedback from people who have what you want. Our friends and our environment often determine our clarity.

Have you witnessed days when the clouds are overcast, and the sky is dark? The day looks dim and blurry. These are days when I keep myself at home and don't move around much. I often get upset when I see this on weekends as I would very much love to get out in nature.

However, sometimes, when we get lucky, the sun rises above the clouds and the clouds disappear, the sky becomes bright blue and the day brightens. This is when I can see further. I can get out in nature and take beautiful hikes, smell the flowers and feel good about the day.

To me, the dark overcast clouds are like friends who are negative. This kind of environment causes us to stay in and not move. The shining sun and the blue skies are like friends who are positive. They bring more clarity to the paths we want to take, and we find it easier to be more adventurous, move out and enjoy the journey.

Reflection: What are the empowering words you can speak over your life? Who are you mixing with? Are they supporting you towards your clarity or keeping you in?

PRACTICAL STEPS TOWARDS CLARITY

Sometimes the root issue of not wanting to answer or decide the next step is that we don't want to take responsibility for our lives. Or perhaps it is fear of the unknown. My encouragement for you is to take responsibility, face your fears, own your decisions and as you learn and re-evaluate, you'll find you, your passions, your purpose, and your clarity. Below are practical steps you can use towards clarity.

1 — BE A GOOD STEWARD

If you are looking for transition, I say this carefully, but we need to learn to be good stewards of our time and finances before anything else. I have had the pleasure of coaching many people. I find that some who are stressed with finances and day-to-day living find it harder to be rational about their decisions, or to even listen to their hearts. Stress and anxiety can drown out your heart's voice. The worst thing to do is to make decisions when you are stressed.

Have you ever worn your glasses in a cool air-conditioned car and then stepped out into the heat? What happens? Your glasses will fog up and it's hard to see clearly.

When we do not have a foundation of basic needs being met, it's hard to find clarity. The glasses often fog up when we step into the heat of survival and anxiety due to lack of funds.

Based on the Maslow hierarchy of needs shown below, your basic needs must be met.

So, if you are in a season of lack, bite the bullet and do what's required and then use your spare time to seek clarity. Trust that this is only for a season. This works out better because when you are doing things outside of your working time, it takes sacrifices. If you are willing to sacrifice your time, that shows that you are passionate about it! That's a great filter.

I shared in the introduction that when I came to Australia, I couldn't find work for the first 6 months. That was when I entered a season of lack. It was very stressful. Now looking back, I'm so grateful for that season. I learnt to live with the bare minimum and set budgets. I went for jobs available which I didn't like, but they paid the bills for a season. Then when opportunity came, I went for jobs I did well in, but wasn't that passionate about. I couldn't see myself doing that for the rest of my life.

It was what I was good at and it gave me the security and comfort to sufficiently make a transition in a few years' time. Small sacrifices in the short term are worth it if it will have a long-term impact.

It was during the season when I had financial security that I started exploring and found my clarity.

2 — FOLLOW YOUR HEART AND DRAFT YOUR VISION

"Everyone has been made for some
particular work, and the desire for that
work has been put in every heart."
Rumi

I used to go everywhere to ask people, to seek their opinion. The more mature ones would say, what do you think? I'd get so frustrated. Tell me! Why are you asking me what I think or what my heart says? Now, I realised what they said is very true, follow your heart.

When I talk to my clients, I often see a reflection of my younger self who didn't even dare to decide what she wanted. Coaches cannot give you the answer because the answer is in you. We can help ask relevant questions. My encouragement again is that if you want to reach higher, you've got to dig deeper – follow your heart, not your mind. Do not compare yourself with others or be concerned about what others think of you.

At the end of this chapter, I have a simple exercise for you to take a look at your possible strengths and write down your vision. This is what I do with my clients at Strengths Based Living evening college in Australia and I have witnessed many clients smile when the "ah ha" moment hits them, when they see how they are uniquely wired for their vision!

3 — FACE YOUR FEARS

"Feed your fears and your faith will starve.
Feed your faith, and your fears will."
Max Lucado

If you have any inclination of what you want to do, face your fears, talk to someone who does it, and just do it. What is the worst thing that can happen? At least you know. Entertain the thought, "What if it is true?" and step forward.

Most of the time, fear is based on self-imposed limitations. Life is already difficult enough as it is; we make it more difficult by imposing limitations on ourselves. Imagine you are looking to climb a mountain, but it looks too big. What do you do? Do you stop or do something about it? Practically speaking, the mountain won't get bigger, but we can get stronger. Facing our fears makes us stronger. The only way you can rise up to challenges is to make yourself bigger. Nelson Mandela puts it beautifully, "The brave man is not he who does not feel afraid, but he who conquers that fear."

I had the opportunity to start a connect group years back and my first response was to say no. The role of the leader is to facilitate, speak and uplift the members who come into the group. Being an extreme introvert, I started thinking about all my negatives like, "Can an introvert lead? Would the members understand my accent? Do I know enough to share? What if no one turned up?"

My mentor saw the potential in me that I didn't see in myself, even though I did dream of being a connect group leader. He always tells me, if an opportunity presents itself before you, step into it! Life often presents itself to you when you are ready to be stretched. At that point of time, I felt I wasn't ready. The good news is that we will never be ready until we step forward! I gave myself permission to say yes and faced the fear, despite thinking I was not up to it. I figured I could learn from it and I had my mentor to guide me. I wish that facing our fears is a one-time thing, but no, it is a daily decision! What kept me going was my vision, which is why we will do an exercise on it at the end of this chapter.

I still remember the first two years were very tough. I always beat myself up after each connect group meeting. I still remember the days I would walk around my home refusing to go to bed, looking at how I could improve! Every week, I feared that no one would turn up! I had to remind myself even if no one turned up, I would stick with it and learn from this process – whether I felt like it or not. Starting something may be difficult but committing to it is the true test! It is choosing to face the fears every day. That is all part of my learning. There is no failure; there are only lessons. Thankfully, the connect group continued to flourish and grew from a miserly 2 people to over 20 people.

Through it, I also learnt how to navigate being a leader and an introvert. I learnt that I had to give space to myself – based on my personality. I have to say no to other stuff so that I can say yes to myself to feed my soul as an introvert.

Now I get to present and speak with audiences of over 100 people regularly in Australia and Singapore. I wouldn't have been able to expand myself and do that if I didn't say yes at the start to 2 people.

I still get shivers, but I'm better at it, I'm a step closer to my goal. Everything can be learnt. When we keep on learning, the task that we fear becomes more familiar, and because of that, we can manage our fears and keep on walking towards our destiny.

"You must take personal responsibility. You cannot change the circumstances, the seasons, or the wind, but you can change yourself. That is something you have charge of."
Jim Rohn

Taking personal responsibility is crucial in order for you to be successful; mediocre people don't ever take personal responsibility for their lives. They just blame everyone else and attend pity parties. At the end of the day, your success is dependent upon you, so rise up and take control of your life.

Your clarity is your responsibility.

Taking responsibility doesn't mean that life will be smooth sailing, but it means that we find the willpower to achieve our goals and not give up.

How our lives turn out is our responsibility and no one else's. I say this again, your clarity is your responsibility. It doesn't matter where we start. Great souls have wills but feeble ones only fantasies. We need to take responsibility to act, rather than playing victim and blaming everyone else. This will separate us from wishful thinkers and pity party goers.

"In the long run, we shape our lives, and we shape ourselves. The process never ends until we die. And the choices we make are ultimately our own responsibility."
Eleanor Roosevelt

5 — ACTION LEADS TO DIRECTION

Take action! John Maxwell, in his book *Talent Is Never Enough*, wrote that there are two kinds of people in this world: those who want to get things done and those who don't want to make mistakes. Which is worse? Not getting things done or making a mistake so that you can learn from it? If you don't want to make mistakes, it's 100% for sure, you won't get anything done, and you won't get anywhere!

In her book *The 5 Second Rule*, author Mel Robbins wrote about how to beat procrastination. She explained that what you do within five seconds of having a thought decides whether or not you will act. Waiting longer allows the mind to dissuade

> Clarity is created through your action.

you often through fear of failure or rejection, or any number of negatives. So take action and work on what you need to do consistently to beat procrastination. Remember, action ALWAYS leads to direction. Clarity is created through your action. It begins with one step at a time. That's your way to clarity, to bringing your vision to reality.

Even Mark Twain once said, 'The dictionary is the only place where success comes before work!' Vision without work is just hallucination.

You may have written down your vision, which is great. Some people spend so much time on the vision but do nothing about it. Writing down your vision is like punching the address in the GPS (Global Positioning System) of your car. However, if you don't start the engine and move, you'll never reach the destination!

I live in Sydney and I often get visitors whom I have to bring out. I often have to check reviews on which restaurants to go to. However, I learnt that not all reviews are accurate! For example, if we are in a small town, the reviews may be fantastic, but this is because it is the only restaurant there. I learnt that as much as I can research how good the restaurant is, I only get the true answer when I have been there physically and have tried the food. That will determine if I will go back again.

How do you know what you love when you have not tried anything? My encouragement is to take baby steps towards what you think you like. Who knows? Maybe you may find it wasn't what you wanted after all. Maybe it could spark something in you that could lead you to your passion!

I have a friend who graduated from Engineering like me. However, as we continued to work, she felt more interested in Learning and Development. First, she started helping her HR colleague in her spare time. She found that she enjoyed it, but still wasn't sure if she wanted to transition. So, she approached her manager to share about her desires and managed to work two days a week in the HR department. The HR department welcomed her as she had been helping them for a while. She tried and realised she loved it! From then, she changed to three days a week and has since pursued her Master of Psychology and has gone on to work full-time as a consultant in Learning and Development. The entire transition took many years, but she wouldn't have stepped into it if she didn't try it out in her own spare time to explore it.

Sometimes the action takes sacrifice, like my friend, she took extra time to help out in the HR department. That could be a very good litmus test to see if it is really what you wanted. If you can't sacrifice time to do it, then perhaps, you just don't like it enough. Eliminate it and move on to what else is in your heart.

6 — BE OPEN

Be open for your dream to take a different form as long as it feeds your vision and energises you. My encouragement is to be focused on your goal but hold on to the process with open hands for it to take a different shape. Step forward and watch how it unfolds.

Be open to be wrong. Constantly re-evaluate as you take mini-steps. It is much better to do something and learn from it than talk about the same thing the following year!

A personal example of mine is that I've always wanted to make a difference. I went to mission school and went on missionary trips. Not only was I having charity fatigue, I was horrible as a missionary!

When I first started out in the mission school, *Youth With A Mission* (YWAM), I started by cooking for others in halfway houses in Malaysia, but I wasn't very effective, as I wasn't a good cook! Two decades later, I realised I can encourage or fund others to go and contribute more effectively than cooking!

Now I am sure, more mouths are fed. I still made a difference, according to my heart's desire, but it looked very different from what I had expected initially. I wouldn't have known these things if I had not taken the first step to go to missionary school even though I felt I failed there!

Have you been on a sailing boat before? They need to plot their overall direction, and then they have to navigate towards it by making adjustments based on the direction of the winds. Likewise, once we have our general direction, then we can re-calibrate by being open to re-adjust.

7 — SURROUND YOURSELF WITH THE RIGHT COMMUNITY

Surround yourself with positive friends and people who have what you want. It will inspire and spark your imagination to see what's possible in you.

No one achieves success alone. We need friends who will encourage us, or even hold us accountable so that we keep on growing. Be open to share your goals and dreams with people who care about you. They will do their best to encourage you and assist you to accomplish them as they want you to succeed too. It means taking a risk as you'll need to be vulnerable in sharing your hopes and ambitions. But it's worth it! A true friend will stay along with you and support you.

8 — FEED YOUR SOUL

Understand how you are wired and what energises you. Remember that in the busyness of juggling work, family, and finding clarity, life can end up very serious and monotonous.

Can I encourage you to take time off to feed your soul? It doesn't need to be a lot of time. Find out what energises you and schedule time for it. For me, because I am wired more to think strategically, I often need time to myself. I schedule time away at least an hour a week to journal and meditate. I create my own retreats. Sometimes it is just time alone to cook; sometimes it is just to run by the waters. It may not necessarily take long. Whatever activity that fills your tank. For some, depending on how you are wired, it may be to spend time with your loved ones. Whatever it is, treasure yourself. Listen to your heart and feed your soul.

I read in *The Barefoot Investor* and even in other financial education resources, they talk about allocating a portion to savings but also allocating a portion for personal enjoyment. I'd like to think that our lives operate the same way too. Schedule time for clarity, time for work, but also schedule time for personal enjoyment. Life is meant to be enjoyed and celebrated. The process will feel a lot easier.

9 — JOURNAL YOUR WAY TO CLARITY

I'd like you to schedule a time for you to dream. Go somewhere where the environment appears limitless with no end, like the sea, the mountains, the blue sky. Take time to observe the beauty of the flowers and trees. Everything you see serves a purpose. There's beauty in diversity. There are different birds, different flowers, different fishes but together they paint a beautiful picture. Even if you don't know what's ahead, believe in this one thing – just as the flowers were colourfully painted and created, so are you. You have been uniquely designed and gifted with talents that will propel you into your destiny if you work on them.

Have a journal to pen your thoughts. Just like when you buy an electronic gadget, there's an instruction booklet, take time to write your own instruction booklet for yourself. Call it a strengths journal or simply label it *Unlocking My Clarity*. If you can find a coach to help you through this process, that's great! But if you can't, I ask you to take time regularly to journal your dreams and what you observe about yourself. No one is judging you; I give you all the permission you need to dream – and dream big.

One of the exercises I often work on with my clients is to understand their strengths, and to draft their vision separately. When you also do this exercise, you'll be amazed to see very often that your vision is aligned to your talents or strengths. Our role is to steward what we have been given to maximise our potential. We are uniquely gifted with the talents necessary to carry out our purpose. Friend, we are good enough!

Yes, we are not perfect, so sometimes we face frustrations along the way. Take them as life-learning lessons. If you can find resources to support you, such as personality assessments or your friend's feedback, it will provide a good starting point. If not, I have a journaling method for you in Exercise 2.1 for you to understand yourself.

The exercises may appear simple or fluffy but stay with me and do them diligently while being honest with yourself at the same time. This will be the start of your journey to self-acceptance and being comfortable in your own skin.

EXERCISE 2.1: DEVELOPING A STRENGTHS-BASED VISION

Helen Adams Keller (June 27, 1880 – June 1, 1968) was a deaf-blind American author, political activist, and lecturer. She said:

> *"The only thing worse than being blind*
> *is having sight but no vision."*

Part A of this exercise is for you to identify your strengths and talents.

Part B of the exercise is for you to draft an overall vision for your life.

A — UNDERSTAND YOUR STRENGTHS

If you are able to invest in a Clifton StrengthsFinder Report, do that to identify your top 5 strengths. This is done through decades of research, so it is very reliable.

If not, you can ask your friends to give you 3 positive words that describe you. Ask as many friends as you can so that it truly reflects you. Collate them and put all words into a word cloud (https://www.wordclouds.com/) to see what the common words are.

Alternatively, you can journal to identify possible strengths. I learnt this journaling method from my mentor, Michael Grinder. Write on the right side of the book and leave the left side blank. Write what you like, what you don't like, what you did, your frustrations, what you enjoy, what you value, and what you are grateful for the day.

Then a few days later, read it as if you are a stranger and observe insights on what you know about the writer of the journal. List this person's strengths and blind spots that you have noticed. Write it in third person using "this person" rather than "I" so that you remain as an observer and don't take it personally. Continue doing this for 21 days, and you'll be able to pick out patterns of strengths or personality, blind spots and values.

LIST YOUR STRENGTHS		
NO.	STRENGTHS NAME	WHAT DOES IT MEAN?
1.		
2.		
3.		
4.		
5.		

B — DEVELOP A STRENGTH-BASED VISION

Think of your personal vision statement before your business one. They should complement each other. Ask yourself these questions:

Assuming time, money, and resources are not an issue, what is it that at the end of your life, you want to look back and be satisfied about?

Alternatively, if you could wave a magic wand, what is it that you want to do?

Close your eyes and imagine yourself as that person you want to be in 5, 10, or 20 years' time. Listen to your heart. Don't overthink this question. Most of us, when we start thinking, we start placing limiting beliefs that hinder us. Just write what comes to mind. Give yourself permission to dream. The more layers you can add to it, the better.
- What is he/she doing?
- Who is he/she with?
- Imagine all the details, including what you wear and what you hear or say.

Then open your eyes and write them down. This is you, who you were uniquely wired to be. Then, based on this picture, what is your vision?

Write till you have a vision that resonates with you so much that you want to do all it takes to reach this vision.

Let this be the vision that drives you.

QUESTION: "WHAT IF I CAN'T SEE MY VISION?"

I believe we can understand our overall vision if we give ourselves the space to ask ourselves without being judgemental. However, there were seasons in my life I couldn't see a vision. Not everyone has a big vision for life. It's okay.

For example, when I first came to Australia and was walking to school to save money, I wasn't in a mindset to dream and think about what I wanted in life. I just needed to survive. At that point, I would say my vision was to get established in Sydney. Our visions can change. Very often, our vision for the future will be enlarged when we reach our current vision. My encouragement is to follow the instructions above and write what you can see at your stage in life now – big or small.

I remember Oprah Winfrey telling a story where she recalled watching her grandmother churn butter and wash clothes in a cast-iron pot in the yard. A small voice inside of her told Oprah that her life would be more than hanging clothes on a line. She eventually realised she wanted to be a teacher, but she said, "I never imagined it would be on TV." Our vision will be enlarged as we step into our clarity.

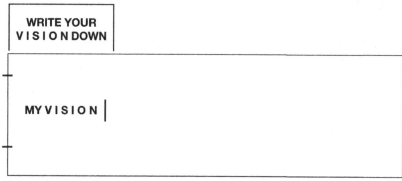

WRITE YOUR
V I S I O N DOWN

MY V I S I O N |

EXAMPLE: WHAT DO I WANT TO ACHIEVE?

Then review both part A and part B.

Very often, you will find that your strengths are very aligned to your end-of-life goal. This gives you the authority to do what you have in your heart! You don't have to compare with others.

Now, craft your vision again and include, if possible, a few of your strengths in the vision. That will remind you that you are uniquely wired to carry that vision!

For example, I personally did all 3 exercises in part A. From that, I noted that some of my strengths are:
- I'm a self starter and an action-taker.
- I am good at strategising for efficiency and effectiveness.
- I am passionate in making a difference in the world.

These strengths were aligned to my vision! You can see my strengths-based vision in the example below.

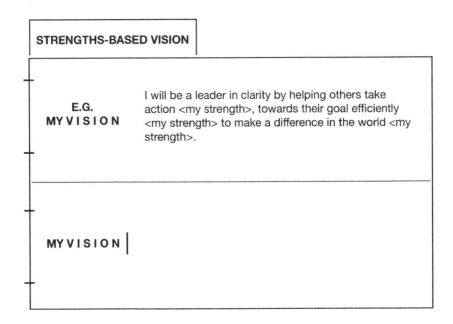

STRENGTHS-BASED VISION

E.G. **MY V I S I O N**	I will be a leader in clarity by helping others take action <my strength>, towards their goal efficiently <my strength> to make a difference in the world <my strength>.
MY V I S I O N	

Chapter 3

STAIRCASE TO AUTHORITY

3 STRATEGIES TO INCREASE YOUR INFLUENCE

CLARITY ALWAYS WINS

———————

"KNOW YOURSELF,
KNOW YOUR OPPONENT,
A HUNDRED BATTLES,
A HUNDRED VICTORIES."

Sun Tzu, The Art of War

CLARITY IS ALSO DEFINED AS FREEDOM FROM INDISTINCT-ness or ambiguity. If you look at a thesaurus, the synonyms of the word clarity include words like distinctness and prominence. Distinctness means individuality, and prominence means eminence or greatness. When we have clarity, we step into our individuality and our greatness! We become free! Isn't that personal authority?

What does it mean to step into our personal authority? Personal authority is where your authority (or right to lead) is instilled by those around you. That's influence, beyond your title or position. Would you like that?

I discovered that personal authority starts with clarity. It is not just clarity about us, but also clarity of those around us so we know how to best influence them.

The quote that best describes strategies for clarity and influence is based on a very well-known military strategist in China called Sun Tzu from 500 BCE. Sun Tzu provided war-winning strategies for the regional state of Wu to win the war against Chu, which was ten times larger in military forces. These war-winning strategies are known as *The Art of War*. He wrote:

"Know yourself and know your opponent,
a hundred battles, a hundred victories."

In the context of influence, I have found that it is a battle of winning people over. Sun Tzu's quote is still very applicable. Your opponent doesn't necessarily mean your enemy; it just means someone you are trying to influence.

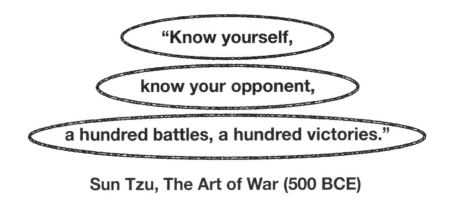

Sun Tzu, The Art of War (500 BCE)

The success of the war starts with clarity internally and externally, and it ends with action. We must consistently apply the strategies to win the battles in our lives.

If you have not heard of Sun Tzu, surely you've heard of the quote: "If you fail to plan, you plan to fail." Did you know this was first quoted by Sun Tzu in *The Art of War*, recorded around 500 BCE?

During the twentieth century, *The Art of War* grew in popularity and saw practical use worldwide. It continues to influence many areas, including culture, politics, business and sports, as well as modern warfare. Sun Tzu's strategies have been mentioned over media and used in business schools and universities such as Yale, Harvard and Oxford till today.

Sun Tzu also wrote:

> "Winning the war with as little combat
> as possible, is the key to true victory."

Stepping up in our personal authority isn't difficult, once we know the path of least combat. This is what I call the path of least resistance to success. Clarity allows us to do just that! This is the path that reaps the greatest return on investment. You do this by tapping into your strengths, something you are naturally good at. This will be the true victory of becoming the best version of yourself, of rising up in personal authority, confidence and influence.

In relation to the art of influence, the staircase to authority consists of three major strategies:

- CLARITY OF SELF (Know Yourself): understand your gifts and talents, your strengths and weaknesses. With this, half the battle is already won. You can create strategies that work for you.

- CLARITY OF OTHERS (Know Your Opponent): your opponent means the people you want to influence, including your customers, clients or even competitors. Understanding them allows you to set effective strategies to influence them.

- CLARITY OF ACTION (100 Battles, 100 Victories): this refers to your battle plan. It is understanding that clarity is a journey and requires action, just like how the military trains for war.

Please see the following Staircase to Authority.

THE STAIRCASE TO AUTHORITY

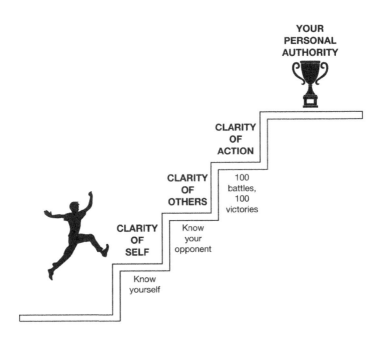

1 — CLARITY OF SELF (Know Yourself)

It is understanding who you are, your strengths and talents, and how you are uniquely wired for greatness. This is the most important first step. Imagine walking through your life with a pair of glasses that are very blurry. You wouldn't dare to take steps. Neither can you see your goal clearly. When your vision is clear, everything becomes clearer and easier.

There is freedom in clarity! Sometimes, it may be better to take a step back, go to the "optometrist" (metaphorically speaking) to understand and find clarity before you continue the race. You don't want to run to the end of life finding out you were running in the wrong race! Once you understand who you are and what you want, your glasses will become very clear. You'll understand what you need to focus on. You will find ease in all that you do, from making decisions to choosing who you want to mix with. You'll find acceptance, joy and satisfaction in your soul, and even have better relationships! Knowing who you can become is indeed the most important step, for clarity is power.

By having personal clarity, you will live for your purpose, not to meet expectations or please others around you. Gandhi once said:

> "A 'No' uttered from the deepest conviction
> is better than a 'Yes' merely uttered to
> please, or worse, to avoid trouble."

You'll uncover your personal why that will propel you forward. Even in business, knowing why is so important. Simon Sinek said:

> "People don't buy what you do; they
> buy why you do it. And what you do
> simply proves what you believe."

Once you come to the belief that you are uniquely wired to carry out your purpose, instinctively it'll give you the drive you need to accomplish what you want. As you uncover your purpose, confidence and authority will naturally follow.

Reflection: How well do you know yourself and your life purpose? Take an inventory of your strengths and even your blind spots and the vision for your life.

2 — CLARITY OF OTHERS (Know Your Opponent)

This is the clarity of others. Your opponent means the people you are looking to influence. It could be your family, co-workers, and even your customers. Yes, you may not necessarily feel so, but you were designed to influence. John Maxwell, author of numerous leadership and influence books, wrote that according to sociologists, even the most isolated individual will influence 10,000 other people during his or her lifetime! To achieve greatness, you must understand it is never about you! It's about others! It will be about the impact and influence you create for others around you. It doesn't really matter to people what you say or do, unless they know what's in it for them. If you want to win others over, or even have a thriving business, you need to know what they want. Profit and influence will naturally follow. People will buy what they want, not what you want them to buy.

Reflection: How well do you know your sphere of influence? What is the value that you bring to people and clients around you?

3 — CLARITY OF ACTION (100 Battles, 100 Victories)

This refers to your battle plan. Very often, people start with dreams and visions, but they never accomplish what they desire. I believe it's not that people do not have clarity. Rather, they didn't have the right battle plan in place to bring their dreams to reality. They didn't act on it. Clarity doesn't come to us; we take action and walk into clarity.

Any battle plan requires action, consistent action. No one wins the war without practice and the daily grind. Do you have a proper plan for action? Have you created the relevant habits to support you? Clarity starts with knowledge but ends in action. No hero is formed overnight. When we see influencers today and all they have achieved, I'm sure they started with something very small. Yet by being consistent to their calling, they have achieved greatness. Mother Teresa was well known for her famous quote,

> Clarity starts with knowledge but ends in action.

> *"If you can't feed a hundred,*
> *you can feed just one."*

She was able to bring in millions and help many children all because she started feeding one child and stuck with it. Consistency also breeds confidence. When you are faithful with the small tasks, you increase your capacity and become more confident. Never wait for confidence to show up. It won't, unless you keep investing in and pushing yourself. If you keep showing up, confidence naturally will turn up. It is now time to shine!

It is hard to achieve greatness alone. You were meant to belong. I noticed all the successful influencers had supporters, mentors and a great team along the way to help them achieve their vision. Helen Adams Keller said:

"Alone, we can do so little; together,
we can do so much."

What about you? What community are you in now? Are they supporting you or holding you back? Do you have mentors or coaches in place to hold you accountable? In your work or business, how is your team supporting you?

Each step will be unpacked in greater detail and explained with examples and exercises in the next 3 chapters.

You'll find that if you do these steps right, in no time, with the right investment in yourself, you'll step into your personal authority with strength and confidence.

EXERCISE 3.1: WHAT'S YOUR CLARITY SCORE?

I derived this from the Balanced Score Card that I use to evaluate suppliers. It helps me to clearly make a decision.

Now I've adapted it to evaluate ourselves, based on the 3 strategies we listed in the staircase to authority. It provides a structure for us to evaluate every goal we make. Perhaps at first glance, it's a lot of work. However, once it becomes a habit, it's very quick. Especially when you get clarity on yourself, each decision will be a lot quicker.

In every task that you do, you can use the clarity score to map out which area you need more clarity. First, list a goal, then ask yourself if you have clarity in each section from 0% with no clarity, to 100% with absolute clarity. Take the average of the 3 sections and that's your average score.

If any of your sections fall below 50%, that should ring an alarm bell. It may be better to find out more first. Clarity is a journey; we walk into it. Start walking and find out more.

For example, I have met:

- People who have created a plan but find it a struggle to execute it because they don't know themselves. They will score low in "Clarity of Self." A proper plan depends on understanding who we are. I've elaborated in the earlier chapter why the HOW to success depends on WHO we are!

- People who have gone on to spend a lot of money and created a product that they love but haven't asked if it was suitable for the market. They will score low on "Clarity of Others." Do your market research first! Whether you have a business, or you want to influence, you have to find out more about the other party.

- People who know themselves well, know their target market but don't have a plan. They will score low on "Clarity of Action." With all the passion but no proper plan, I have seen some crumble in anxiety, especially when there is a financial impact. Then, my encouragement is to get a plan created. Perhaps we need to give ourselves more time and grace, to make it more practical and to reduce the level of stress.

YOUR CLARITY SCORE CARD

YOUR CLARITY SCORECARD	
WRITE DOWN YOUR GOAL(S)	**DATE**
SCORING CRITERIA	**SCORE (0 - 100%)**
CLARITY OF SELF Do you know what your strengths, values, vision and mission are? Is this goal aligned to your vision?	
CLARITY OF OTHERS Do you know who the people you need to influence are? Are you addressing their pain point? How much do you know what their values, strengths, wants and desires are?	
CLARITY OF ACTION Do I have the right habits, friends, mentors to support my goal? Do I have a battle plan?	
AVERAGE SCORE	

YOUR AVERAGE SCORE	COMMENTS
0 - 50%	You need more clarity. Ask yourself, which areas can I get more clarity? I will have exercises in the following chapters for you to work on to achieve better clarity. Be very careful whom you ask to seek clarity as it may leave you confused. Get someone knowledgeable you can be accountable to. Give yourself grace and time to find clarity. I believe in you.
50 - 85%	Good! You are on track. But you can be better. Ask yourself, what are the areas in each section you can work on to increase the score. I believe the exercises will provide you greater clarity and motivation. Also, you can get a buddy or someone to be accountable to, to keep refining it. Sometimes, it is just some tweaks that can make a huge difference!
> 85%	Congratulations! Go for it! Perhaps look at ways you can fast track the process. Be bold to articulate your goals to others and get a buddy or someone to be accountable to, to keep refining and re-evaluating your plan as you go along. Read on to see if you can develop strategies to fast track this.

Chapter 4

CLARITY OF SELF

YOU ARE UNIQUELY WIRED FOR GREATNESS

CLARITY REVEALS OUR GREATNESS

"I PRAISE YOU FOR
I AM FEARFULLY AND
WONDERFULLY MADE,
YOUR WORKS ARE
WONDERFUL, I KNOW
THAT FULL WELL."

Ancient Psalm
(written around 1048 BCE)

HAVE YOU EVER FELT THAT THE MORE YOU SHARE YOUR dreams and visions with your friends, the more confused you get? Sometimes, trying to seek a suitable path for yourself ends up with analysis paralysis. It pushes us into immobility just because we cannot tell what's right or wrong for us, so it seems safer to remain status quo.

Sometimes, we may not get the support we need to pursue what we want to do, so we don't take action. However, life continues and is not satisfying, and we start searching again. The whole cycle repeats itself sometimes to the point that we believe we have been dreaming too much and accept life as it is.

I have been through that cycle many times. I have found that to break out of it, to understand your dreams and visions, it is important to find clarity – based on how you are uniquely wired. Clarity as a verb is to clear, which means to eliminate ambiguity or doubt from a matter.

I'm here to remind you that we are all different! This means, when you ask your friends and family, be aware that they are seeing through a different lens from you. Imagine getting several opinions from differing views; it can sometimes be very confusing and disempowering.

So hold on to the strengths-based vision you've created in the earlier chapter and keep on ploughing and moving towards it!

YOU ARE UNIQUELY WIRED

Imagine yourself as a bag of coins. In this bag, not all the coins are equal; there are gold coins, silver coins, and copper coins.

Traditionally, when we do not know what our talents are, we usually like to work on our weakness. It is like picking out the darkest coin (obviously copper) and working hard and investing time to polish it. However, while effort allows the coin to shine, the value remains as copper. We see improvement but not as much as we had hoped for, plus it takes a lot of effort. There is a limited return on investment.

Any assessment is simply a tool to help you identify the gold coins that are already in you. They are the start of your clarity journey. When you work with your talents, gifts and strengths, they will reap the greatest return on investment. This is what I mean in finding your path of least resistance. If someone told you that you can shortcut your path to success by picking out your gold coins, would you not do that?

Not only that, when you operate from what you are good at or when you are doing what you are passionate about, it will energise you. Have you sometimes felt that you are in the flow when you are doing something, and you forgot about time? On top of that, you get more energised. These are the gold coins in you.

These gold coins could already be very polished and shiny. This means that people around you may notice that you are good at these things. Your strengths represent your gold coins. Or sometimes, they may appear as blind spots that need a bit more polishing.

Make it your philosophy to focus on what you are good at rather than what you are weak at, in order to maximise your potential. With the correct strategies and investment in place, you can identify your gold coins and find strategies to polish them to shine their best.

Understanding that we each have been gifted with a different set of gold coins helps us not to compare with one another because we are all uniquely different. It helps us focus on what we have and make our set of gold coins shine.

Yes, you were made to shine. You are good enough! Stay in your lane, look not to the right or left, for if you try to be someone else, it drains you. Look at the gold that is already in you and let's work on it together. It's now time for you to shine. Remember that a synonym for clarity is prominence; having clarity allows us to see our personal prominence, our personal greatness. You are uniquely wired for greatness!

Friends, my encouragement to you is to stop discounting yourself, or thinking that you are not good enough to carry out your dreams and visions. You have been uniquely wired to realise these dreams. I hope this itself gives you the freedom to pursue your heart's desire – with wisdom, of course.

Do not worry about skills; skills can be learnt. Our potential, the eventual quality of our skills, is really up to us. Our role is to walk our path. Then steward the gold coins that we have been given to carry our purpose and maximise our potential.

CLARITY IS A MATTER OF PERSPECTIVE

"To know thyself is the beginning of wisdom."
Socrates

To illustrate how perspective is essential to clarity, let me share with you my personal story. I'm being open and transparent here, and I hope this can illustrate why our perspective matters.

I grew up doing fairly well in school. Back in Singapore, I was blessed to have gone to the top schools. Life had been comfortable even in my career; I never had to interview for work, I was often referred to my next role, and I have been blessed to work with big multinationals and on exceptional teams.

However, when I came to Australia to do my MBA, there was a season I could not find work and I found myself having anxiety attacks. I was also unfortunate to live in an area where I had racist remarks spoken over me. It didn't happen often, but it wrecked my confidence. On top of that, I was often rejected at work, even in administration and waitressing jobs, as I could only work 20 hours per week. I felt the lack of confidence and I became socially awkward. Being someone who wanted to address the issue, I sought help from a psychologist. It was then that she diagnosed me with Asperger Syndrome (AS), a developmental disorder characterised by significant difficulties in social interaction and nonverbal communication, along with restricted and repetitive patterns of behaviour and interests. It is a milder autism spectrum disorder.

I was shocked to find out that I was mildly autistic. Suddenly, all my previous accolades appeared to be part of this new negative label. She told me people in the autistic spectrum can be very smart. I was always academically very strong, and I used to be proud of it. But now, carrying that label of AS, I hated what I used to be proud of. I wished I was "normal" or "average."

She told me I had to take depression medication to cope with the pressure of finding work. So I did, since I needed the energy to look for work, but things kept spiralling downwards. The side effects of the medication made me more socially awkward as I would get an upset stomach, so I kept to myself most of the time. I used to enjoy going to places with friends on camping trips, or to stay over in holiday homes over the weekends, but I stopped.

I still remember walking into the chemist like a zombie looking to pick up my medication, talking in a slur, and being very inefficient. I remember running away from relationships thinking I was not good enough.

I asked the psychologist why she diagnosed me with AS, and she said those with AS are people who see things as black or white. Hence, they have difficulty in handling situations when things don't go their way, especially in relationships. They will struggle in social situations where it is not a purely black or white matter. She told me being mildly autistic, I may have to take the medication for the rest of my life.

When I found a job that was a good fit, I was ready to stop the medication. I asked if there were alternatives to medication. She said I could try to cope with exercise, be conscious of my negative feelings, and push through. But life would be difficult.

I felt crushed. I didn't know what to do. I didn't dare share with my family because I felt so much shame.

The turning point came when I watched A *Beautiful Mind*. This movie was inspired by events in the life of John Forbes Nash Jr., and in part based on the biography A *Beautiful Mind* by Sylvia Nasar. John Nash was a mathematical genius; he made an astonishing discovery early in his career and stood on the brink of international acclaim. But Nash soon found himself on a painful and harrowing journey of mental issues and self-discovery. The movie showcased him learning to cope with his illness. He took his medication, but he could still see the hallucinations. True relief came when he accepted it and took responsibility.

I went to my psychologist again. It was on that day I made a decision to walk out and learn to deal with it rather than rely on medication. Don't get me wrong. I believe that there is a time when we need to take medication for certain conditions that we may have. However, I personally didn't think that was a long-term solution for me.

Ever since I was diagnosed, I spiralled downwards and reflected more symptoms of AS. I never felt like that till I was diagnosed. I took on the label and it became my reality. I was happy before I was diagnosed. I wanted to go back to my happy self.

I chose to take responsibility for my life. If I decide not to take medication, then I must take care of my health and learn to cope. I decided to cope through healthy eating, through seeing a Chinese herbalist, and having consistent exercises to increase my endorphins. I came off the medication slowly and assimilated back to life. Life was okay, I found a good job and years later started a connect group that was flourishing.

However, the label stuck with me. Whenever I got into some conflict in relationship, I would dish out that label as an excuse. It became my crutch. It stuck with me for many years, affected me in my friendships and even relationships. I would often walk away, thinking I was not good enough to be loved.

It felt that since I was labelled with AS, I started wearing a new pair of lenses that was permanently stuck on me. I kept seeing shame, not good enough, and self-pity wherever I went. Outwardly, no one could tell, but inwardly, I was crumbling.

What about you? Are the lenses you are wearing causing you to crumble? Are there things that make you feel so shameful that you have never told anyone?

I tried very hard to shake it off. At times, after going to a positive seminar, I would tell myself this is it! No more self-pity! I will be positive. It felt as if I took off the glasses and stomped on them. Enough was enough! I felt good for a while. I learnt to make positive affirmations. It worked for a while, but I felt something was missing.

Whenever I bumped into issues, especially in relationships, I'd crawl back and put on the glasses again, as an excuse. This time, they looked worse as I had stomped on them! There were cracks in the lenses and life looked dimmer.

The worst place is the in-between, the in-between of the past and the present. I felt stuck; I would take a step forward, and then a step back and put on the cracked glasses. It was safe; it was my crutch, but every time I picked up those glasses again, life looked way much worse. It made me feel helpless and hopeless. What if my condition was true? I could never break away, no matter how hard I tried. That was how I thought.

Do you sometimes feel trapped between negative and positive thinking? Do you sometimes feel that your positive thinking backfires and leaves you in a slump?

Fortunately, I had a lot of loving friends and mentors who kept reminding me not to wear the label. Others asked me to see another psychologist to get a second opinion. Maybe I was in denial, but I didn't want to see another one. I was scared. What if the other psychologist said the same thing? I would have to relive and feel the shame all over again.

True revelation and liberation came when I did my Gallup Clifton StrengthsFinder assessment. It described the blind spots of one of my strengths as a tendency to see things in black or white. That was the very reason why the psychologist diagnosed me as having Asperger Syndrome(AS)! Finally

I realised, it is just a blind spot. Nathaniel Branden was a Canadian American psychotherapist and writer known for his work in the psychology of self-esteem. He said, "The first step towards change is awareness. The second step is acceptance." I learnt to accept my blind spot and work with it and didn't let it define me any longer.

CLARITY TRUMPS POSITIVE AFFIRMATIONS

That was when I learnt that clarity TRUMPS positive affirmations. In some personal development courses, we've been taught to think positive and declare positive affirmations about what we want. However, if our underlying belief is contrary, it often backfires. I think that was what happened to me. I could say outwardly all forms of positive affirmations, but if inwardly, I still saw my AS label, I'd still spiral towards feeling not good enough.

Zig Ziglar, a well-known American author and motivational speaker said this: "It's impossible to consistently behave in a manner inconsistent with how we see ourselves. We can do very few things in a positive way if we feel negative about ourselves." We can't outperform our self-image. The lens of poor self-image has to be completely broken.

Finally, understanding the symptoms that the psychologist defined as Asperger Syndrome was just a blind spot in my personality, I found clarity. With absolute clarity on how I am wired, this pair of glasses that trapped my life is now completely and fully broken.

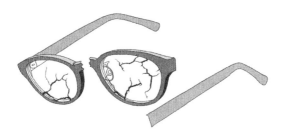

The label finally came off. I felt the weight fall off my shoulders. I felt so relieved! I felt that the shackles that had chained me were finally broken!

Perhaps it was a misdiagnosis since I was in a new culture in Australia and was trying to adapt. Or perhaps it was true. Even if it were true, I have learnt to look at the positive part of it. I started designing my own new glasses to wear, so that I can move towards where I want to go, just the way I am. Some call it re-framing; I call it a brand-new frame!

This pair of designer glasses is better than the top brands, because it is fully customised for me and I make a conscious choice to wear them every day. I call this brand – greatness. Not only does it give me laser sharp vision, I think it makes me look much better too!

I had to create a new perspective with a new lens. Can I encourage you to create new lenses and change your perspective in life and win? Yes, let me use how I'm wired to my advantage.

Now my positive affirmations align with my clarity; with clarity comes power to propel me towards my destiny. I stopped seeing myself as a victim and stopped having my own pity parties!

The following are my examples of positive affirmations, and I encourage you to develop your own to replace your once negative beliefs, according to your strengths.

I am intelligent - since people with Asperger Syndrome are usually very smart, I remind myself I have all the intelligence I need to pursue my dreams. I can always learn what I don't know and find a way to achieve my goals.

I can selectively choose to be black or white – my strength reminds me I have core unchanging values. I now use it for my advantage. I follow the quote, "If you think you can, you can. If you think you can't, you can't." So, I choose to think I can and go after my dreams. I hold on to my strength-based vision and know that I am uniquely wired from heaven to carry out my vision. That is my authority! Why should I care what others say? How about you? What do you tell yourself?

> Clarity trumps positive affirmations.

It actually doesn't matter if I had AS or not; I do not have to carry the label and behave like there is something wrong with me and feel sorry for myself. I am free to be me, free to pursue my dreams – the way that motivates me, based on how I am wired.

Sometimes I wonder how many people are diagnosed and labelled just because they were operating in their blind spots! I also wonder how many people beat themselves up based on the unnecessary labels and stop pursuing the dreams in their hearts.

Clarity is not about looking somewhere else; it's about having a new perspective, a new lens that looks at your strengths, and motivates you towards your dreams.

Find a coach if you can, to help prescribe you a new lens that works for you, and not against you. It's time to change your lens. Find clarity to break off the old negative labels; destroy those glasses completely. Wear new ones!

Don't compare your path with others, because we are all uniquely wired; we all have our own paths to our destinies. At least at the end of the day, you can assure yourself you have tried your best. We learn about ourselves not by what the label says, but by how we respond to things; we can correct it, review it and be better.

> Strive not for perfection but step into your greatness.

Don't strive for perfection, because we will never be perfect. If you do, you will always end up disappointed. Strive not for perfection but step into your greatness.

Mother Teresa said, "I can do things you cannot, you can do things I cannot; together we can do great things."

Yes, together we can do great things. We just have to do our part. We are not only uniquely wired; we are uniquely wired for greatness.

YOU WERE BORN FOR A PURPOSE

Do you know what's your purpose? Your WHY must be big enough for you to make the necessary sacrifices to achieve what you want and find success. Passion is more important than a plan. It is the fuel that allows you to keep on going, so as to eventually reach there. It is the difference between people who achieve their goals and people who don't. Find the sweet spot of WHY that will propel you to success.

There have been teachings that we need to find our purpose before we move; however, not everyone knows what their purpose is right from the start. Plus, life evolves and changes too quickly; it can be hard to determine your purpose right

Your purpose unfolds as you move forward.

from the start. I firmly believe your purpose unfolds as you move forward, towards your passion, as you understand the areas you are willing to pay the price for.

Purpose in life is far more important than property or possessions. Having more to live with is no substitute for having more to live for.

Nelson Mandela was a South African anti-apartheid revolutionary, political leader, and philanthropist who served as President of South Africa from 1994 to 1999. He was the country's first black head of state and the first one elected in a fully representative democratic election. How did he achieve what was seemingly impossible at his time? He had a priority and paid a huge price, but he achieved his vision. He said this:

"Vision without action is just a dream, action without vision just passes the time, and vision with action can change the world."

A top management consultant once said, "No chief executive was ever fired for lack of vision." But many are unable to put their vision into action. Visions don't work unless you do.

What do I mean by that? Simply put, find a WHY that's big enough for you to pay the price and persevere to reach the goal. If you are not willing to pay the price, chances are, you haven't uncovered the real WHY. I find that very often, inaction is just a sign of the lack of clarity. When our WHY becomes clear, it propels us to greater action.

The exercises at the end of this chapter will give you some structure to find out your WHY.

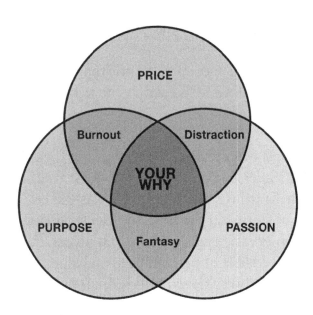

Your true WHY is likely one that aligns your purpose and your passion and something that you are willing to pay the price for.

When you have passion and purpose, but you are not willing to pay the price for it, it remains as a fantasy. Let go of it and move on.

When you are willing to pay the price for something that aligns with your purpose, but you are not passionate about it, you may suffer burnout. It may be better to outsource that task or learn to enjoy it.

> Inaction is just a sign of the lack of clarity.

When you are passionate about it and are willing to pay the price for it, but it's not aligned with your purpose, check if that becomes a distraction. It could be a hobby, which is great! We all need to feed our souls. However, when we become too obsessed with it, something else in our lives will have to pay the price for it. Prioritise it accordingly.

Sometimes we cannot see how we can be paid for our WHY. It's okay. We can distil our WHY first and then re-evaluate on how it can align with our vocation.

It is hard to find out your purpose and passion by doing nothing. Action leads to direction. Or are you looking to please others and doing things based on others' opinions of you? If so, then it may take a while to uncover your true purpose and passion – not what others think of you.

Maybe you don't have clearly defined goals yet, but there are distinctive things you do where you enjoy and feel "in the flow" and things you do out of obligation and duty. You can start by identifying what you are passionate about. Sometimes, opportunities present themselves for you to develop your passion. Step into them. Why not? Say yes and regret later (if needed). That's a great way to test your passion!

When one is driven by purpose, passion, and pays the price towards it, there will come a time where there is a tipping point, where everyone else comes alongside with your vision. Never underestimate the day of small beginnings.

When you discover your true WHY, setbacks won't hold you back, and you are prepared to count the cost. Understanding your purpose will empower you; through that, as you stretch towards it, it will enlarge you. As you share your passion with others, you'll rally a community who will support you. Keep taking action and investing in yourself, and you will definitely turn your talents into strengths.

Have you heard of TED Talks? TED (Technology, Entertainment, Design) Conferences LLC had a single mission – to freely distribute online "ideas worth spreading." The founders, Harry Marks and Richard Saul Wurman, believed passionately in the power of ideas to change attitudes, lives, and ultimately, the world.

In the fall of 2012, TED Talks alone (not including TEDx, which are independent presentations similar to TED in presentation) celebrated its one billionth video view. As TED Talks continue to be watched around the world, with an average of 17 new page views a second, in over 100 languages, TED conferences and events continue to inspire, motivate and thrill attendees.

Did you know that the very first TED lost money? If the founders had not persisted, it would not have had the influence it has today. The history of TED is published on their website (https://ted.com).

TED was born in 1984 out of Richard Saul Wurman's observation of a powerful convergence among three fields: technology, entertainment, and design. The first TED, which he co-founded with Harry Marks, included a demo of the compact disc, the e-book and cutting-edge 3D graphics from Lucasfilm, while mathematician Benoit Mandelbrot demonstrated how to map coastlines using his developing theory of fractal geometry.

But despite a stellar line up, the event lost money, and it was six years before Wurman and Marks tried again. This time, in 1990, the world was ready. The TED Conference became an annual event in Monterey, California, attracting a growing and influential audience from many different disciplines, united by their curiosity and open-mindedness—and also by their shared discovery of an exciting secret. (At the time, it was an invite-only event).

Meanwhile the roster of presenters broadened to include scientists, philosophers, musicians, business and religious leaders, philanthropists and many others. For many attendees, TED became one of the intellectual and emotional highlights of the year. That was certainly true for media entrepreneur Chris Anderson, who met with Wurman in 2000 to discuss the conference's future. A deal was struck, and in 2001, Anderson's non-profit Sapling Foundation acquired TED, and Anderson became its curator.

In making the conference non-profit, Anderson stood by the principles that made TED great: the inspired format, the breadth of content, the commitment to seek out the most interesting people on Earth and to let them communicate their passion. It soon became clear that the ideas and inspiration generated at TED should have an impact well outside the city limits of Monterey.

Now there are also numerous TEDx programs, independently run programs springing up across the world. It all started with a vision: a passion to spread ideas. It cost them time, effort, and even money. But they never gave up because the WHY was big enough, and they were willing to pay the price.

Passion supersedes talent, because passionate people will keep on going and paying the price to be better. In due time, they will outperform those with greater talents. I'm sure there were better event organisers who could run things more smoothly, but they never created something as impactful as TED.

It doesn't mean that you have to turn your passion into your career. It gives you clarity to steward your time and resources more effectively. Perhaps you can look at aspects of your passion and apply it in what you do. Be open as you explore. Steve Jobs went for a calligraphy class in college, which he later credited to be the inspiration for Apple's beautiful typography. Don't rationalise yourself out of your interests! You may never know where it would lead.

Life can appear dry if we live without passion; it can run like clockwork, and it may feel like going through the daily grind of life just to survive. We are made to flourish and shine. Sometimes it takes risks and we need to pay a price, but at least it brings us a step closer to our dreams. You want to walk to the end of this life and look back and say, "I have done what I was born to do." If not, we can only live a life of regret. Which is worse? Taking risks and knowing, or feeling safe and you are left wondering?

There may be times you do want to transition into what you are passionate about. If you can make a living from that, great! Be practical and responsible towards yourself and others as you take steps towards it. Passion alone cannot feed us,

Passion supersedes talent.

but if we know the price we need to pay, even if we stay in a job we are less passionate about to pay the bills, we will become less resentful at work, knowing that this is just for a season. Remember, clarity is a journey! Keep walking towards it.

Even the ancient Chinese sage Confucius said this centuries ago,

> *"Choose a job you love, and you will never have to work a day in your life."*

In the book *If It Ain't Broke, Don't Break It!*, Robert J. Kriegel and Louise Patler wrote about a study they did based on 1500 people over 20 years. They discovered that people who chose their passion ended up earning more money than those who chose a path just to earn money.

There will be an exercise at the end of this chapter for you to reflect on what your passion and purpose could be.

UNCOVERING YOUR PASSION, PURPOSE AND PRICE

If you know your passion and purpose, great! If you don't, give yourself grace and time to uncover them. It may be nearer than you think! You just need to take more action to find out.

EXPLORATION, EXPERIMENTATION, EXECUTION (3Es)

To make things easy to understand, I liken uncovering your passion to dating. You don't fall in love with the first date. However, if you don't go on dates, you won't fall in love at all!

Finding your passion is the same; try what you are interested in for a few times and see if the passion grows. Take it that you are dating yourself, to discover yourself.

Our hearts are way smarter than we realise. Our hearts are our internal GPS. Sometimes we make a wrong turn; what does the GPS do? It beeps and alerts us. Likewise, your heart will tell you if it is what you love, only after you move. What happens when we don't hear from the GPS? There are only two possibilities: either we haven't started the engine, or we are on the right track! Perhaps you are already in your passion and purpose! Only you can tell. If there is nothing else you want to try and experience, perhaps you are already in what you love.

> Our hearts are our internal GPS.

When you see that and take ownership of it, imagine the joy of waking up each day to do what you love and knowing you are on earth for a reason. Seek then to think: what else can I learn to make me better in what I do?

Do you remember I used to run a connect group and dreaded it? Because growing and stretching was uncomfortable. But I soon realised that I was willing to pay the price for turning up every week. That was when I realised that witnessing people grow was my passion! I realised it was time to shift my focus to look out for areas where people grow instead of focusing on the growing pains. Nothing changed, but I enjoyed what I did a whole lot more. Let us be that great unselfish self, progressing to make a difference.

So how do we apply the 3Es to find our passion? To put it simply, these are 3 phases. The 3Es will help you filter out the WHY that you are willing to pay a price for.

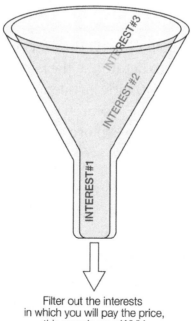

Filter out the interests
in which you will pay the price,
this reveals your WHY

1 — EXPLORATION

You go on the first date, to determine if you want to meet the person again (not marry him or her!) – that's exploration. Too often, we are too scared to make a move because we think we need to know the end result. No, if that's not true in dating, that's also not true in your life. When a man dates a woman, he seeks to find out what she likes to eat and what activities she likes, just so he can take her to places she enjoys, right? Sometimes he takes her to a new place she hasn't been to before and she ends up enjoying it. Great! Take it that you are dating yourself to find out what you like. It's okay to make mistakes. What's the worst that can happen? Move on. Likewise, do whatever is on your heart. Once you start doing them, it will become clearer if you enjoyed doing that. By exploring and doing the activities you think you are interested in, you get to learn to follow your gut or to hear your heart. The voice of your heart will become louder. Making decisions will become easier.

Some people would analyse till they feel paralysed. Without exploration, it's hard to determine the answer. But as you keep on exploring, it will come fairly instinctively. It's like purchasing a home; you can do all the research you want, but most of the time, once you step in and explore a bit, you'll know if it is the home you want. You've got to step out and step in to what you think you may love.

2 — EXPERIMENTATION

You then go on a few dates and see if a deeper connection develops – that's experimentation. You may meet a lot of people, there will be some you don't want to meet again, there'll be others you don't mind meeting again. Likewise, filter a few interests you are keen to proceed with and get deeper with them.

It is hard to determine what your passions are until you give it a go. Sometimes you may need to stick with it before you enjoy it. For me, I love tango, but it's very technical. For the first few sessions, I hated it, but I loved to watch my coaches dance. That motivated me to keep learning. Now I enjoy it. Don't rule yourself out if you are still learning and there are some skills to master. Knowing that action always leads to direction, soon you'll be able to identify what are the interests you are willing to pay the price to continue.

Don't stay in this phase for too long; quickly eliminate and continue. It's like dating. It's hard to date too many people at the same time for too long!

3 — EXECUTION

Finally, you get exclusive, meaning you cut off seeing all other partners and focus on one – that's execution. What are the few things you are passionate about and want to focus on? Focus on what energises you and then make a decision. This will be the sweet spot of the WHY that you are willing to pay the price for, even at the expense of giving other things up.

If you are looking to transition into a different vocation, it can be tough and tiring, especially if you are choosing between a job that pays the bills and your passion. Remember your vision will be your anchor to move you forward. Also, sometimes it may be a season where you must do something you are not exactly passionate about to bring in the income. It's okay!

Give yourself grace and a season to explore, experiment, and finally make a decision to follow through and execute. Then don't look back! Keep moving forward till you receive momentum. Remember that starting is always the toughest!

When I first transitioned to be a coach, it was tough. I saw people who used to report to me rising and climbing up the corporate ladder. Yet, I was starting off in something new, I had irregular income. I had to keep going back to my vision and reminding myself it is only a season. I also had to make practical choices, for example, cutting down my expenses while my business grew. This, too, will pass. At least I am working hard for my life's satisfaction. I choose to be true to myself, listen to my heart and follow my passion. I was willing to pay the price because I found my WHY.

What about you? Have you found your WHY?

EXERCISE 4.1: DEVELOPING 3Ps

*"A great leader's courage to fulfil his vision
comes from passion, not position."*
John C. Maxwell

Answer the following questions and list the concrete steps you can do to start exploring.

PASSION

What do you sing about?
What do you cry about?
What do you dream about?
What are your interests?

PURPOSE

What do you do that makes you feel most alive?
What are you excited about?

PRICE

Prioritise your list of passions above based on the price you are willing to exchange for it and start exploring!

From your passions that you are willing to pay the price for, ask yourself why you are doing that and how it is aligned to your purpose.

Compare these with your vision and start to think about what you can do to align your passion, your WHY, with your vision.

Revisit this after 3-6 months and re-evaluate those questions again. Some interests may fall away now that you've tried them. If you can't bring yourself to try an interest, possibly you are not passionate about it at all, so strike it off the list.

I say this respectfully, if you have a New Year's resolution that appears every year, but you did nothing about it, strike it off the list. You didn't want it enough to pay the price. De-clutter and focus on what matters most.

EXERCISE 4.2: STORIES, STRENGTHS, SKILLS (3Ss)

"He who knows others is wise;
he who knows himself is enlightened."
Lao Tzu

We are who we are today based on how we are naturally wired, and also based on what we've learnt and experienced through our lives. Our purpose very often comes from the stories in our lives and the strengths we carry. This exercise will help give us a snapshot of who we are, based on our stories, strengths and skills.

1 — STORIES

Go to the table on page 119. Write down your life stories, things that you remember the most. List the major highs, the lows, and the turning points that impacted you. Alternatively, they could be the things you love or find yourself repeatedly doing, which reveal your passions. They usually end up being our life's purpose. For example, I have met women who had been abused in the past and want to help others who have been abused. I've met people who ran a successful start-up and want to help other start-ups to flourish.

Write down 3 - 5 stories/passions in your life during different stages of your life from past to present.
- What did you learn from the story?
- What did you love about the story?
- What skills and capabilities did you see in yourself?

- What core beliefs and values have helped you navigate through these seasons?

Then go take a break, have a cup of tea, go for a walk or leave it for the next day. After that, return to your stories.

Review your stories and see if you can add anything else to them.

For example, in the table on page 119, you can see my stories has 2 highs and 3 lows. What does yours consist of?

When I first came to Australia, it was a low point of my life (point 4), but through it, I learnt a lot. I'm now obsessed with helping others find clarity because of that! When I found my clarity and transitioned, it became high (point 5).

UNDERSTANDING MYSELF
(3Ss EXERCISE)

STORIES | Write down 3 -5 major turning points or passions in your life from past to present.

N O.	
1 .	
2 .	
3 .	
4 .	
5 .	

E.G. My stories

Your stories

2 — STRENGTHS

Strengths generally refer to a person's character, how they think, feel, or behave. They usually shine through the pivotal moments of your stories. It is quite innate and individualistic. For example, you notice that a child displays certain characteristics at a young age, without needing to be taught. Strengths could be qualities such as resilience, positivity, an analytical mind, a visionary outlook, a strong-willed personality, being responsible, and so on.

In the table on page 121, list at least 5 strengths you see from Exercise 2.1 in Chapter 2 on page 71. Next to each strength, write down a possible corresponding blind spot.

For example, my very first role required me to travel to different cities to help start the offices around Asia. I was a pioneer. In other words, my strength was that I'm a self-starter. I can deal with ambiguity and start projects. However, because I started things so quickly, my blind spot was that I became impatient and didn't bring people along. I was then responsible for managing the Taiwan office. I had to take time to communicate effectively to both the US and Singapore offices. Starting a business in a new country took longer.

For a period of time, I was blaming myself for the delay. I wished I knew that was my blind spot then. It would have saved me a lot of sleepless nights! Blind spots are not bad. They can be overcome; we just need to be aware of them and be trained, like in driving, to look at them. Think about how you can overcome your blind spots.

3 — SKILLS

A skill is the ability to do something well. These are things that can be learnt, such as typing skills, accounting skills, negotiation skills, speaking skills, basketball skills, etc. List down in the next table, the skills you currently have.

**UNDERSTANDING MYSELF
(3Ss EXERCISE)**

STRENGTHS///////////////////////BLINDSPOTS

1.		
2.		
3.		
4.		
5.		

SKILLS/

1.	
2.	
3.	
4.	
5.	

Go back to your vision; then ask yourself:

- How do your stories fit in and support you in your vision? What can you share with the world based on your stories?
- How did your strengths and blind spot support or hinder you in your stories?
- What are the additional skills you need to achieve your vision? Or perhaps who have the skills you need?

Do not compare yourself with someone who is better than you and discount yourself. Your stories are unique to you; your strengths are unique to you; and whatever your vision and purpose are, you can always learn the skills needed!

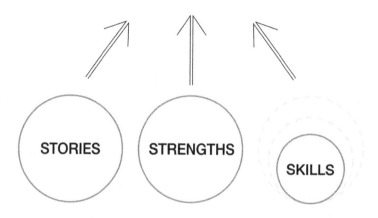

Don't ever rule yourself out just because there are things you need to learn. People will come alongside you and help you. Alternatively, you can partner with others who have those skills that you need. That's the best part!

Additional skills you can learn:

1.
2.
3.
4.
5.

People you can partner with:

1.
2.
3.
4.
5.

Then schedule yourself action items with investment (time and or money) and a start date to learn the skills. Alternatively, share with the people you've identified, those with the relevant skills regarding your vision.

Chapter 5

_____

CLARITY OF OTHERS

UNDERSTAND HOW TO INFLUENCE

CLARITY ALWAYS ADDS VALUE

———

"YOU WILL GET ALL YOU WANT IN LIFE, IF YOU HELP ENOUGH OTHER PEOPLE GET WHAT THEY WANT."

Zig Ziglar

JOHN MAXWELL ONCE MENTIONED THAT ACCORDING TO sociologists, even the most isolated individual will influence 10,000 other people during his or her lifetime!

Influence means having the power to have an effect on people or things. It means to affect or change how someone develops, behaves, or thinks.

It's about having clarity of others. If the other party is your spouse, then he or she will better understand your intention and support you. If it is your team, bringing them to your side allows them to support you and increase team engagement. If it is a client, it may even mean more revenue!

Jim Rohn is an American author, entrepreneur and motivational speaker. He is known to have mentored many to fame, including motivational speaker Tony Robbins, Jack Canfield (*Chicken Soup* book series), author/lecturer Brian Tracy and T. Harv Eker. Jim Rohn said this,

> *"You don't get paid for the hour. You get paid for the value you bring to the hour."*

Clarity of others allows you to not only effectively communicate with them, it also equips you with the ability to understand how you can add value to them. Clarity is like a diamond; the more clarity you have of yourself and others, the more value you can bring to others!

Why add value to others? When you can add value to others, you not only receive the satisfaction that you are impacting someone's life, you also get respect and trust in return. In terms of negotiation, you can establish a win-win situation that works for both parties.

Albert Einstein once said, "Only a life lived for others is a life worthwhile." You may have also heard different people quote this: "If service or adding value to others is beneath you, then leadership is beyond you." We cannot avoid step 2 of the staircase if we want to step up in our leadership and personal authority.

Along with greater influence, you may receive criticism. Rick Warren, in his book *The Purpose Driven Life*, has pointed out, "Criticism is the cost of influence. As long as you don't influence anybody, nobody is going to say a peep about you. But the greater your influence ... the more critics you are going to have."

This is why the first step in the staircase to authority, clarity of self, is so important. With personal clarity, you will stand your ground because you know who you are. Remember, clarity is POWER.

"All warfare should be a warfare of intellect," Sun Tzu said in *The Art of War*. He continues, "It is more important to outthink your enemy, than to outfight him." He also adds, "So, in war, the way is to avoid what is strong and strike at what is weak." This can be reflected in how the Chinese play the game of Go or "Wei Qi", which is similar to a board game like Chess.

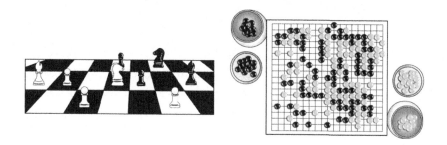

In Chess, for one party to win the other, they need to kill the opponent's king, usually leaving few of the opponent's pieces on the board. In Go, the objective is to conquer as much ground as possible. Understanding the opponent doesn't mean killing the other party all the time; it means conquering more ground, perhaps going to places your enemy is not at.

Both Chess and Go require one to:
- Predict and anticipate the opponent's move. Having clarity of your opponent's thinking allows you to more effectively predict, anticipate and win.
- Decide what move to take.
- Re-calibrate based on opponent's response. Sometimes, even if we don't have a clear strategy, we just need to figure out the next step to improve our position.

This is similar to us in life, while searching for clarity. Chess pieces each have a specific special power, but in Go, you don't need any special power to win. You can simply win by strategy, by gaining territory as quickly as you can. For example, if you have a business, what are the niches you can go for quickly where your competitors are not there yet? Understanding the opponent literally drives your strategy. Understanding who you are determines how you will execute your strategy.

How do you outthink the people you want to influence? I believe it begins by understanding who they are, what they want and then creating a win-win situation for all parties. Influence isn't about one party winning and the other losing. It's about both achieving their individual outcomes. The more parties there are, the more we need to spend time to think and strategise.

What if you knew what your client, your customer, or the person you want to influence wants or what their next move might be? Would it be easier for you to influence the person? What if you knew your client's pain points? Would it be easier to sell them the solution? I'm sure it would be.

As a consultant, I was often thrown dead projects, meaning the company had tried ways to salvage it but in vain. In the last attempt, they send it to an external consultant. For this particular project I was given, they had been having issues with a fuel supplier in another country. The company always had a problem paying the supplier in time, and the supplier would always threaten to stop the supply. This fuel was used to generate electricity in the camps, so the company could not afford to have the supplier cut the supply. This had been on-going for 4 years and the contract was expiring soon in the next year. Almost every month, you would see the finance team running around like headless chickens trying to manage cashflow and ensure payment was done. It meant special exceptions from the CEO himself as it was a huge lump sum of money.

When I came on board, I simply observed their communication with the supplier. The supplier didn't have English as their first language. I sensed a lot of hostility between both parties. They had been asking the supplier to accept longer payment terms but in vain. I was told to handle this going forward as the people on the ground had tried everything they could.

First, I got to know our operations, to understand our consumption patterns, so that I knew the minimum extra I had to order to ensure the camps had the fuel they needed while we arranged payment. That's the first step of the staircase to authority (Clarity of Self). For the second step (Clarity of Others), I had to quickly do some research on this supplier, using the client avatar exercise at the end of this chapter. What is he like? What are his values? What are his frustrations? What are his pain points? I also had to find out who the key decision maker was so that I could speak to the person who could change the situation.

Then I dropped him a call, greeted him in his language and apologised for causing so much grief; that was when he started complaining and mentioning all the problems that had happened.

Have you ever received negative feedback or complaints? I used to be upset about it; now I learn to see it as feedback for me to get to know my clients better.

Abraham Lincoln said, "I don't like that man. I must get to know him better." Benjamin Franklin said, "Love your enemies, for they tell you your faults."

Surely, for such intense animosity, we must be at fault too. There must be something we can correct to make the other party happier. As I kept listening, it dawned on me their major frustration was that they were worried that we wouldn't pay them, or we might choose another supplier after the current contract ended. Clarity of others requires us to tune in and listen, to hear their hearts.

I also noticed that the person valued family and respect. Based on this information, I drafted a proposal for him. I placed a guarantee that we would continue working with him and would also give him recommendations. Understanding that he valued respect, I took time to explain to him respectfully, to demonstrate that we were doing our best to pay him, but our internal process was the bottle neck, not us. After much discussion, we managed to set up a win-win situation where he received security to be our preferred supplier and we received security of consistent supply. What they couldn't do in 4 years, I managed to do it in 2 months, thanks to Sun Tzu for his strategy that works all the time!

> Clarity of others requires us to tune in and listen, to hear their hearts.

Perhaps you don't know exactly who you are looking to reach. There are general trends we can look at to find a few tips. It's important we understand how tomorrow's world will look like. It will be overcrowded with information. Attention spans are getting shorter. People are more visual. There is a lot of information fighting for our attention. The key to grab attention is to be specific to what people want, to be concise, short and sweet with our messages.

I use this even to communicate with my 12-year-old niece! She lives in a very different world than I! I struggled getting to know her, until I got to know what she liked. I had to watch K-pop singers, to find something to talk to her about. Do you have people who are very different from you, but you want to connect with? Understanding what is important to them is the bridge that connects.

Consider a man courting a lady. Would he not do what he could to find out what hobbies she has, in order to strike a conversation with her? Would he not find out what food she likes, so that he could bring her to lunches and dinners she would enjoy? Influence is not difficult; we do it naturally, it just requires us to be intentional. Unfortunately, in life, sometimes we get bogged down by tasks or by just wanting to win, to be right, such that we forget to think about the other party. Be intentional to know the other party and understand the value you bring.

Influence is never about you! It's about the other party. It's about how we can add value to the other party. It's about how we can support the other party. It's about how we can make their lives better. That is the foundation of all relationships, be it in career, business or family.

It doesn't even matter if the other party is very different from you. Given the right strategy, you can still win them over. Sometimes through this exercise, you determine this is not the partner you want to work with after all. Then, it's okay to walk away with your head held high since you've done your homework.

What if you feel small and like you have nothing to add value to the other party? You'll have to think creatively to set your strategy.

Being a procurement professional, it's easier if the supplier spends a lot with us. They treat us like kings and always give us the best; that's because they don't want to lose their biggest source of revenue. If there is a limited supply, we will be the first clients to get it.

However, what if we are just a small client? It doesn't matter if they retain our account or lose it; it makes a minimal difference to their revenue. How do we get the attention and the level of service we need? How do we win them over? That's when we need to ask: is there something we can give them so that they can value us as a customer in return?

I remember negotiating with a large catering software company. They had huge clients ranging in the hundreds of thousands to millions in Europe. We were only spending slightly less than $100,000 with them, plus we were in Australia, which made it very difficult for them to service us. It was also difficult to get their attention.

After much discussion, we realised that because we were the first few in Australia who used their software. Others were coming to us to ask about their software. So, we offered to co-develop case studies as part of their promotional materials to expand their markets in Australia. Because of that, they made sure we got the best service as other companies who receive the case study may call us for feedback. It is still possible to win, regardless of where we start, no matter how small we are. Sun Tzu in *The Art of War* reminds me of this.

Sun Tzu was able to conquer his opponent who was 10 times larger by using this strategy. "Avoid what is strong, strike at what is weak." That's clarity.

The question is: "How well do you know the other party?"

KNOW THEIR WHY

Understand that at every exchange, the other party always wants to know what is in it for them. It's never about you! No one cares about you unless it is made relevant to them. Until you answer the magic question for them: "What's in it for me?"

If this is a business, then we need to specifically target the right market, understand their pain points and solve them. Then, we will have a client and sometimes they become our friends.

Below is an exercise to find clarity of others. You might be familiar with it; it's a modified version of the client avatar. Once you find clarity of others, it will help you to influence others. If it is a business, it will help you strike win-win situations in negotiation, or even give you ideas about what your marketing strategies could be.

EXERCISE 5: DEVELOP YOUR CLIENT AVATAR

This is an exercise to determine your client avatar. If you know the person, put down his/her name and details. If it is a market you are after, you can personify them to get an idea of who your targeted customers are.

You may have come across many different client avatars, but based on my negotiation background, I'd like to add in one more question: "What can you give to the other party that will make a difference in achieving what they want?" In short, what is the added value you can give them?

> To be able to influence and strike a win-win, give first.

For example, based on the chapter above, I gave the software company case studies, and in return, I got the service I wanted. Approach the conversation with the aim to give, not just to get. Give, and you shall receive.

To be able to influence and strike a win-win, give first. It may not cost you much, but it makes a difference to the other party. Trust that out of reciprocity, the other party will return the favour and join you in the win-win situation. Even if they don't, you've left a good impression.

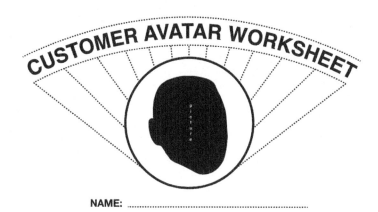

CUSTOMER AVATAR WORKSHEET

NAME: ....

AGE: ....

GENDER: ....

MARITAL STATUS: ....

CHILDREN: ....

JOB TITLE: ....

EDUCATION: ....

GOALS AND VALUES	CHALLENGES & PAIN POINTS

SOURCES OF INFORMATION	OBJECTION & CURRENT ROLE
Books: Magazine: Website: Social Media: Who does the person follow? Hobbies or spends time on:	Possible objections: Role: Who is the key decision maker?

What's in it for this person/market?

Based on the above, what added value can I give the other party to strike a win-win situation first?

1.
2.
3.

Chapter 6

CLARITY OF ACTION

CRAFTING YOUR BATTLE PLAN

CLARITY IS CONSISTENT ACTION

"I FEAR NOT THE
MAN WHO HAS
PRACTICED 10,000
KICKS ONCE,
BUT I FEAR THE
MAN WHO HAS
PRACTICED ONE
KICK 10,000 TIMES."

Bruce Lee

A LOT OF PEOPLE THINK THEY NEED CLARITY BEFORE THEY move. I have come to learn that clarity is action done consistently. The first 2 steps in the staircase to authority are not enough without this third step.

I personally believe it's not that people do not have clarity. They have dreams and aspirations, but these remain as fantasy because they don't take action. It is the third step of the staircase to authority that is pivotal to bring their dreams to reality. A battle plan. Action. Consistent action. Do you have clarity of action?

Jim Tressel is an American college football coach. His teams earned several national championships during the course of his career, earning him numerous accolades. He wrote in his book *The Winners Manual*:

> *"The hallmark of excellence, the test of greatness, is consistency."*

To step into your greatness, you require consistent action. A simple example is if a person wants to lose weight, after he or she has found a suitable exercise and diet plan, action needs to be applied consistently to see results. This is the same with everything else. Clarity begins with understanding and ends with action – consistent effort to produce results.

> Clarity begins with understanding and ends with action.

Unfortunately, we all know for a fact, gym membership sales soar at the start of the year but many members stop going to the gym after a few months. These people never get to reap the results they wanted.

The good part is that if we are consistent for a certain period of time, once the first sign of results is seen, the goal becomes way clearer and more achievable. The more consistent you are, the more clarity you get, the easier it gets! Your clarity becomes clearer as you consistently take action. How cool is that?

The question is: "How consistently are you working towards your goals?"

I heard of a story of two brothers who decided to swim across to a nearby island to play. They had been practicing and swimming every day, so as to swim across to the island that was only 200m away.

Both jumped in and started swimming. The elder brother swam without looking back and reached the island. When he reached, he couldn't see his brother anywhere. Finally, he realised that his brother was back at the shore where they started from. He asked his brother, "What happened?"

His brother said, "I swam midway and as I looked back, I realised how far it would be if I had to swim back. I was afraid I couldn't make it to the other side, so I turned back."

The elder brother said, "Why do you think this way? If you look back, you'll find that you'll always be further and further away from the start. I chose to look forward and see that I'm getting nearer and nearer to the shore I want to reach. That motivates me and keeps me going as I know I have not much more to go before I reach it."

Both planned and trained together, but one reached the goal, and the other didn't.

Which brother are you? Are you someone who meets an obstacle, becomes afraid, resigns himself to fate, and turns back? Are you someone who prefers to go back to your comfort zone? Are you anticipating failures more than you envision success?

It didn't matter if the younger brother was stronger or even faster; the sad part is that he didn't make it to the other side, because he wasn't consistently working toward his goal. He turned back.

Many times in life, those who achieve their dreams may not be the fittest or the strongest; they are the ones who have the grit and consistently work towards their goal. John C. Maxwell even wrote a book called *Talent Is Never Enough* to remind us of this fact. In one of his *Minute With Maxwell* videos, he said it beautifully: "Grit always wins over giftedness." People with potential may not realise their dreams, if they don't invest consistent effort to bring it to reality. Talent is like a seed; you know it can grow into a magnificent tree, if you plant it in fertile soil, and water it

> Your clarity becomes clearer as you consistently take action.

consistently. However, if you don't water it consistently, it remains a seed, small and buried underground.

Cartoonist Charles Schulz said, "Life is like a ten-speed bike, most of us have gears we never use." Understanding your talent is a great start, but not enough, unless you work towards your dream.

Or are you like the elder brother? Once you've set the goal, you'll do what it takes to reach it. He looked ahead and saw that he was nearer to the shore. He used that to encourage himself to keep going. Are you someone who is tracking and celebrating your progress, motivating yourself toward your goal?

If you want to develop your talents and turn them fully into strengths, you don't begin by just focusing on your talents. No, you start way before, by tapping into the power of your mind. If you expect to fail, then you will. But if you expect yourself to succeed, and work on it with bulldog faith, then success is just around the corner.

You may have heard of Sir Roger Gilbert Bannister (23 March 1929 – 3 March 2018). He was a British middle-distance athlete and neurologist who was the first to run a mile under 4 minutes. In the past, no one believed they could run a mile under 4 minutes, so no one did. However, he believed he could, and he did it. The interesting thing was that right after he did it, many others followed; there was only a 46-day gap. Why? Was it because they became stronger supernaturally? I don't think so. They always had it in them, but the missing link was their expectations. Now that someone else had done it, they gave themselves permission to believe and expect that it was possible.

Are there limiting beliefs you have placed on yourself? Do you want to be like Roger Bannister and expect bigger things?

What's interesting to note is that Roger was a neurologist; he wasn't even a full-time athlete. This means there is capacity in you to pursue your passion while maintaining your profession if they are different. There is always more in you than you might expect. You always had it in you. These talents were with you right when you were born. Can I encourage you to expect greater, and know that you've got more in you? You can break records – the records of your own limitations in your mind, if only you believe.

Roger made history, always being noted to be the first to run the "Miracle Mile." Many others came after, but no one remembered them. Worst of all, perhaps there were many who were born to do so but never did. Who do you want to be?

Battles are inevitable. There are different battles to fight. The very first key to winning the battle is to believe that you'll win. Plan to win and win it in your mind first.

Once you have decided, the one that keeps on going towards the goal wins. That's consistency in action. Even Mother Teresa said, "I do not pray for success, I ask for faithfulness." She knew if she were faithful to her task, she would find success.

Talent is like a seed; if you water it consistently, you may not see much for a while. But slowly and surely, it can grow into a tree that can bear fruit and provide shade to others. I believe that was what Mother Teresa did to accomplish so much in her lifetime. She was faithful with the small consistently and the big came.

Sir Winston Churchill has been described as Britain's greatest leader ever. I read that when he returned to his old school, Harrow, to address the boys, the whole school assembled to listen to his words of wisdom.

His speech has been put all over the web as something short like this: 'Never give up, never give up, never give up.' The actual words of the salient portion, from *Churchill by Himself*, is as follows: "This is the lesson: never give in, never give in...in nothing, great or small, large or petty—never give in except to convictions of honour and good sense. Never yield to force; never yield to the apparently overwhelming might of the enemy..."

Mistakes do not matter as much as giving up!

Churchill made mistakes; he failed at times, but he never gave up and, in the end, he is still called Britain's greatest leader. Mistakes do not matter as much as giving up! Why do we fear making mistakes or failures? We should fear more about giving up!

Peggy Noonan, speech writer for Ronald Reagan, America's 40th president, and political columnist for *The Wall Street Journal*, spoke of courage, but not without noting its underlying foundation in consistency.

"Part of courage is simple consistency."
Peggy Noonan

Once you've done your due diligence and have made that plan, it often takes great courage to follow it consistently. It doesn't matter how insignificant it may feel. As long as you persist, it will lead you to the mountaintop after wading through the valleys.

Consistent action doesn't mean being stubborn and inflexible. It means we consistently work towards our goal; we consistently refine and review our plans and work towards our goal.

Even America's 34th president, Dwight D. Eisenhower said, "In preparing for battle I have always found that plans are useless, but planning is indispensable."

We plan as much as we can and we must remain nimble to respond, so as to win the war, to achieve our goal.

KNOW YOUR BATTLES

Having talent is not enough; we need to work on turning them to strengths and to achieve goals in life. There are different types of battles we need to be aware of. Understanding them will help us prepare ourselves. Even if we have the best product or message, if we are not prepared, we will not win the game.

Norman Schwarzkopf commanded Operation Desert Storm, successfully driving out Saddam Hussein's Iraqi forces from Kuwait in 1991. He said:

> *"The truth of the matter is that you always know the right thing to do. The hard part is doing it."*

If you don't act, dreams never become a reality. They remain a fantasy. For a caterpillar to transform into a butterfly, it recognises it must spin a cocoon around itself and live a boring, stationary, dark life for a period before it becomes a butterfly. No one likes mundane training. But to experience the exhilaration of winning a war, every soldier must put up with the grind, going through mundane training before he or she goes to war. Unless one waters a seed consistently, the seed will never grow into a majestic tree. All potential seems small at the start, but as we feed it, we will watch it grow.

No one is as interested in you getting paid, doing well, and reaching your potential as you are. Sometimes, people put too much emphasis on the coach. As a coach or mentor, we can show the way, we can discuss what to do, but ultimately nothing happens until you decide to roll up your sleeves and get into the action. If you want to get ahead, you need to light your own fire.

Above all else, ensure that your battle plans are aligned with your vision. Having talent without focus is like pulling a boat in all directions. The sad thing is that it may end up stationary with no progress. Without a clear focus or direction, it's hard to be an expert in an area. We may be busy, but we may not produce results. That is why clarity of self and clarity of others is the foundation to our battles. A focused beam of light through a magnifying glass can spark a fire. When you are focused, people around you can tell and can get behind you to support you. Remember, you are not fighting this battle alone.

To describe why having battle plans are important, General Norman Schwarzkopf said:

"The more you sweat in peace,
the less you bleed in war."

There are different battles we need to prepare for. I've categorised them into 3 groups.

1 — DAILY BATTLES

*"The secret of your success is
determined by your daily agenda."*
John C. Maxwell

It is about winning daily battles to achieve your goal. This requires focus and discipline till they become habits. Success is a result of good habits over a period of time.

*"If you don't program yourself,
life will program you!"*
Les Brown

As long as we master what we do every day and create supporting habits, we will master our goals. Be faithful with the small and the big will come. We progress based on the decisions we make each day.

The difference between first place and second place in any sport is just a matter of seconds. Don't underestimate the daily grind and improvements that make you shine. A little extra effort always gives a person an edge over others. Very often, we see a successful person and think he or she is lucky. We fail to see the hours he or she has put in prior to that.

Ignacy Jan Paderewski was a Polish pianist, composer, and former prime minister of Poland. He said:

"If I miss one day of practice, I notice it.
If I miss two days, the critics notice it.
If I miss three days, the audience notices it."

What I find helpful is to create a daily or weekly schedule on what you will do every day to ensure that you carve out time to develop the daily habits. Create the best practices for yourself. When are you most creative? When are you most productive? What can you create in your daily habits that you can get in the zone all the time? For me, my mornings are my most productive and creative time. I know I get more creative after an exercise! So I schedule my mornings to exercise, read and learn before I start the day for work. I also schedule an hour before bed to read, reflect and write my grateful journal. What about you? You can only build momentum on what you have planned. Once you've scheduled, then hold yourself accountable to stick to it!

Reflection: *Do you know what are your daily habits that will lead you to your success? I also encourage you to journal every day to reflect and refine the habits that work for you.*

2 — PLANNED BATTLES

Planned battles are the ones we can prepare for. When you bushwalk, you enter the forest after you have the map. Likewise, have a map before you go for your life's battles. Your path may change but you need a plan. Then take courage to start, practice, and demonstrate pure perseverance to conquer it. What are the daily habits you need to help you towards your planned goal? Then work it backwards and ensure they are in your daily battles. Play to win! Plan well!

Abraham Lincoln said:

"If I had 8 hours a day to chop down a tree,
I'll spend 6 hours sharpening my axe."

Regardless of what you do, you can visualise it and train your mind. You must believe in yourself and what you are doing. Sometimes the preparation process is long and slow. It may require formal education. It may require you to find wise mentors. It may mean getting out of your comfort zone. Or it could mean simply fine-tuning a skill you've nearly mastered so that you can get to the next level. But whatever it requires, remember that you must be ready when your time comes.

Sometimes you have to review your plan and re-calibrate accordingly. What I find helpful is to regularly schedule to meet with your CEO. Who is your CEO?

If you are the owner of your life, who is the CEO? Yes, YOU. Take yourself and your life seriously. If you don't, who will?

When you meet with your CEO, imagine yourself in five years' time living the life you want, then bring this future self back as your CEO and meet with him/ her. Discuss what needs to be done to become the future that you see. Discuss your personal Key Performance Indicators (KPIs) and track them. Identify road blocks. Sometimes it may also mean letting go of things that take up your time but doesn't contribute to your future. Clarity is to understand what's holding you back. Then discuss with your future self on how to overcome it. Develop wisdom

> Clarity is to understand what's holding you back.

by overcoming these roadblocks in every area of your life –
emotionally, financially, socially, physically and spiritually.

*Reflection: How often do you meet with your CEO? Score your-
self 1-10 regularly on how you are tracking. How often do you
review and re-calibrate your plans? For me, I meet my CEO
every Sunday afternoon over a nice cup of tea to plan the week
ahead. I also have a longer meeting every quarter to review and
re-calibrate.*

3 — UNPLANNED BATTLES

Roman philosopher Seneca reminds us that we make our own
luck by staying prepared, he said:

> *"Luck is a matter of preparation
> meeting opportunity."*

There are unplanned battles in life for which we need to rise to
the occasion. Opportunities don't come often, but when they
do, are we ready to take them up? The only way it can be done
is that we are consistently preparing for it. This highlights the
importance of continual learning and practice that will make
a difference when opportunity comes.

I recall in my younger days, I used to train as a gymnast. I
was not as strong, but I trained with friends who were. My
friends were selected to represent our school. I was not. I was
very disappointed, because I wanted to compete. I continued
training with my friends as I enjoyed their company, but I
was not taking my training seriously. One week before the
competition, my friend sprained her foot, and the coach asked

me to take her place. I was shocked. I was not prepared and declined. In the end, my friend went ahead for the competition with a sprained foot instead. For me, I lost the opportunity to compete, simply because I wasn't ready. I realised my dream was to compete, but I was not willing to prepare myself. That dream remained a fantasy.

I learnt that I shouldn't have let my training be dependent on circumstances – whether or not I was selected to compete. I learnt that I should approach life in whatever I do, with the intention to better myself. When the opportunity comes, I would be ready.

Were there opportunities you lost, just because you were not ready? Do you have the intention to better yourself so that you remain prepared for what may come?

Sometimes the opportunity, the unplanned battle comes disguised as a crisis. Especially now, at the time of writing, the world is facing the crisis of an unprecedented pandemic of COVID-19, there are so many disruptions to our lives and a lot of unknowns, worldwide. How do you see crises?

Sometimes we are met with a crisis in life, we go through a season of shaking and disruption. But it is at those times, just like mining gold, the shaking causes the gold to be separated from the dirt. Have faith, perhaps this could be the time you get to declutter and find your clarity. Perhaps new doors of opportunity could open up for you.

In my early days in Australia, the entire procurement team I was working in, was made redundant in 2 days. Close to a hundred of us lost our jobs. It was a nerve-wrecking season.

I saw a lot of people getting into panic for different reasons, including myself. Fortunately for me, I had saved a bit of money, and I also had other income such as renting my extra room out, so I was able to use the time to learn some things while contemplating the next step.

When the crisis happened, I realised I was grateful that I couldn't find work when I first came to Australia! It was those bittersweet days where I had learnt that my identity was not tied to what I do. Through the years, I was fortunate to have found a group of very nurturing friends, so when I lost my role, I was a little more prepared emotionally.

When I caught up with ex-colleagues a while later and they asked me what I was doing, I just joked and laughed, "Oh, my part time job is to wash and change bedsheets (for my Airbnb clients)!" My identity is not tied to what I do; it is tied to who I am. It doesn't matter what I do at that moment. I know this is for a season; I have to be practical and be a good steward of my finances and time, knowing that this season will pass. There's power in clarity. Thank God I had already started on the journey to know myself to prepare myself for this crisis. Understanding who we are prepares us for the unprepared battles that may come our way as well.

It was through this season that I decided to start my own consultancy practice. It was scary to start but I have never looked back. I was very blessed to get good clients, better revenue, and I could even take more time off for vacation and to visit my family in Singapore! Through the crisis of being made redundant, came the opportunity that changed my life! The practice had served its purpose until I fully transitioned to coaching in 5 years.

How prepared are you for unplanned battles that come your way? A key litmus test is to understand if you are constantly learning towards your overall vision.

Reflection: *Are you learning and growing towards where you want to be?*

YOU WERE MEANT TO BELONG

To win battles, you do not fight alone. Your victory depends on who you surround yourself with. Sun Tzu said, "He will win whose army is animated by the same spirit throughout all its ranks." We need to put proper strategies in place so that we can play to win. This is a very simple but crucial strategy.

No one achieves successes alone. We need friends who encourage us, mentors or coaches to hold us accountable so that we can keep on growing. As you share your goals and dreams with people around you, some may even come alongside and fight together with you. It does mean you have to be vulnerable in sharing your hopes and ambitions. However, if you are truly passionate about it, surely you'll pay the price to voice it out!

The people you choose to mix with can make a huge difference. They can paddle with you in the same direction or drift you away from where you want to go. I remember going kayaking with friends. We thought, we'd head out and paddle for a while, relax, and then easily paddle back. Little did we know that we drifted so far away from the starting point, my friend had to get to the shore and run to ask for help. This was only one day. What about many of us who live every day with no intention?

Before we know it, we are a lot further away from where we had wanted to go.

I also remember going on a kayaking expedition with friends, where I followed my friends towards our camping spot. It was tough work to catch up, but we had direction. When we reached our camping spot, we could laugh and celebrate with each other our accomplishments. Do you shun away from friends who may stretch or push you?

William Clement Stone was a businessman, philanthropist and self-help book author. He said:

> "Be careful the environment you choose for
> it will shape you; be careful the friends you
> choose for you will become like them."

Don't hang around people who seek to belittle your dreams. That's a waste of your precious time. Seek to befriend people who inspire you, challenge you, lift you higher, and make you better. Great people make you feel that you too can become great. Choose to hang out with the visionaries, the believers, the doers and the courageous.

Build a community that will make you better. Lead and care for the people below you, laugh and support people who are your peers, and learn and stretch with the people above you.

I have seen introverts come alive and get energised when they are speaking from their passion. Likewise, working with people with the same cause and passion can energise you. Imagine if you surround yourself with a group of people who have the same passion and purpose, do you think you'll find more energy to walk a second mile and achieve success? That's the power of community.

The question is: "Who are you consistently mixing with?"

We need generals (mentors or coaches) to guide us and for accountability. This is because feedback is important and helps us to accelerate our growth. We also need a team of soldiers (community) to fight and practice together. We need the right community for us to flourish because you become who you mix with. If talent is a seed, then to me, the community is fertile ground, mentors and coaches are like fertilisers. When the seed is planted into that fertile soil, with regular nutrients, the seed will grow into a strong and healthy tree. Provided that it is watered consistently, which represents consistent action.

Now that we've walked through the staircase to authority, you may be thinking, "Ruth, it sounds too simple and theoretical; plus, you don't know my situation. I don't have much to start with." My encouragement is that it works, regardless of where you start. Let me share with you this story.

I first met Siew May at our speaking events. She was born with a condition called cerebral palsy, a disorder that affected her speech and her control of some body movements. Because of her condition, she spoke in a slur, and I almost couldn't understand her. But she persisted and I finally understood. She said, "I…. want…. speak…. betttteeerrr." I loved her determination and positive energy. I saw courage, conviction and clarity.

Then she handed me a book she wrote, entitled *Scaling Walls*. I was so very humbled and impressed! At that point of time, I was hoping to write this book and came up with all sorts of excuses and blaming everyone around me with reasons why I hadn't completed it. Yet, I met Siew May, who had completed hers and she gifted it to me.

Have you ever procrastinated and come up with excuses for not doing the things you wanted to do? Have you talked about something you want to do but never got to doing it? Or are you like Siew May, who pursued her dreams without caring what others may think?

On the bookmark that came with the book, she wrote: "If I kept comparing myself to others, I will always be unhappy." What a timely reminder for me to stop coming up with excuses and comparing with others! I had to be reminded of what I preach to others! That was indeed humbling, a very sobering wake-up call for me.

The following picture shows Siew May and I'm holding her book.

I knew I had to interview Siew May, about how she wrote her book, and what she did and how she was so clear in what she wanted to achieve in life. I knew this would inspire many.

The average sales of a self-publisher is actually just 250 books. Guess how many Siew May sold? Siew May in her consistency has sold over 10,000 books! Not only that, she also regularly gave talks in schools and other corporate places including Google office, JP Morgan and Prudential. She was featured in local newspapers and on television as one of the unsung heroes in 2014 and also as one of Singapore's silent heroes in 2017.

That happened over a period of 10 years. She never gave up. She did not let her disability stop her. She said at the Silent Heroes Awards in 2017, "As long as we have a life, we can create miracles with our love for others and live life to the fullest."

She, to me, is one who has applied all three steps of the staircase to authority and has stepped into her personal authority. She found clarity of self and others, and most importantly, she found clarity of action. It didn't matter how she started; she surrounded herself with the right community and worked consistently to achieve the outcome she wanted. When one steps into their personal authority, confidence comes. Her speech may not be as clear, but she shone with confidence when she spoke.

If you are looking to increase your confidence, don't focus on confidence itself. Focus on stepping up the staircase of authority. Focus on finding clarity, in yourself and your targeted sphere of influence, and consistently practice towards your goal. Confidence will turn up when you turn up daily to fight your battles.

So, how did Siew May do it?

Siew May was the youngest of a family of five children. Despite financial and family difficulties, she still managed to complete school and achieved her N Levels certificate, which is similar to a high school certificate. She grew up in a time when she had to face social prejudice as a disabled person. It was difficult for her to find work and assimilate into society. People sometimes avoided her and called her an alien because she looked different.

She shared with me her vision, "I want others to know that being disabled doesn't mean we are un-abled." She wants society to accept the disabled and she also wants to encourage other disabled individuals to face their fears, to go out and to lead normal lives. This means, she first had to face her own fears and live the life she wanted others to have.

She didn't start off so confident. She used to be very fearful about going out into the world. She hated the looks she had to face and the treatment she received for being different. It was when she attended a course from Asia Works and found a community who believed in her that she found the confidence to step out. With the group supporting her, she managed to write her first book and stepped out to speak.

Was it easy for her to start? No. She had a lot more barriers than most of us. Not only was she disabled, her family conditions were not favourable. Neither did she start with much money, as it was difficult for her to find work to sustain herself, let alone write and publish her book. Yet, she never gave up. She stood tall because she knew who she was; she surrounded herself with people who supported her.

Over 10 years later, she achieved what she set out to do. A lot of us see the final result of the successes of others, but we don't see the sweat and the hard work they put in before their success came. Siew May worked hard consistently to achieve all these. She had the energy to keep going as she was clear about her life purpose.

What about you? What excuses do you have? Are you willing to work hard towards what you hope to achieve? Clarity becomes more evident when you work hard. Like I mentioned before, if you want to lose weight, the first few months of exercise are the toughest. But when you see results, it gets easier. It becomes way clearer that you *can* achieve your goal. Likewise, don't be disheartened, keep on going. Do it in faith that results will come as you keep turning up each day. If you find it tough, remember Siew May.

> Do it in faith that results will come as you keep turning up each day.

I asked her if she is going to write another book, and she said yes immediately. "What's the title of your next book, Siew May?" I asked inquisitively and she said, "Never Give Up!" What a qualified person to write this! She is a walking testimony of one who never gave up.

It's time to lay down all excuses, it's time to stop comparing, and it's time to get into action. A step at a time, consistently towards our goal. Siew May slowly but surely, took over 10 years to sell over 10,000 books. She has achieved something great by being faithful to her tasks, telling her story one at a time, a word at a time.

If you want to support Siew May by purchasing her book, you can write to scalingwalls.siewmay@gmail.com to place an order.

So, what's your next step? Do you have a battle plan? Is your community supporting you or tearing you down?

These was a very famous poet called Li Bai in the Tang Dynasty in China (701 - 762 BCE). He was known as the Immortal Poet. He served the Tang Emperor as a court scholar. A legend was told that when Li Bai was young, he was naughty and didn't like to study. One day, while he was playing by the river, he saw an old woman grinding an iron rod on a big stone. It caught his attention and he went up to the woman and asked, "What are you doing, granny?"

The old woman kept on grinding the iron rod while she answered, "Grinding an iron rod."

He became curious and asked, "What for?"

She replied, while still grinding the iron rod, "To make a sewing needle."

Li Bai laughed and replied, "The iron rod is so big, it will take many years to make it a needle!"

It was this answer that changed his life. She said, "This doesn't matter at all. As long as I persevere, there is nothing I cannot achieve."

Li Bai realised her wisdom and went back to school. He decided to make the effort to study and became a skilled poet. He came up with the Chinese idiom, "If you work at it hard enough, you can grind an iron bar into a needle." Li Bai ended up working as a scholar for the emperor. Perseverance will cause one to be skilled. Being skilled, we can serve before kings.

Even the ancient proverb says:

> "Do you see a man skilled in his work?
> He will stand before kings; He will
> not stand before obscure men."
> Ancient Proverb (700 BCE)

Perhaps you feel your dreams are too far and hard to reach. My encouragement to you is to simply take the first step. It may feel uncomfortable. Perhaps people will laugh at you saying you are wasting your time. Keep on going. Your clarity will become clearer as you master the skills you need. Perseverance always pays off.

Just like Li Bai, you can change your destiny with a decision. Just like Siew May, you can use what you've got and propel yourself to your destiny and achieve greatness. Keep on going. One day you will serve before kings.

I believe in you.

EXERCISE 6.1: DETERMINE YOUR ALLIES

CONSIDER YOUR COMMUNITY

List the people that you spend the most time with. Have an honest review if these people can support you to reach your vision you listed in Exercise 2.1. Are they providing you feedback, and connections based on your client avatar in Exercise 5? If not, explore where you can plug yourself into a new community that's positive and supportive.

My current community:

1.
2.
3.
4.
5.

Possible new communities and actions:

CONSIDER YOUR MENTOR(S) AND COACH(ES)

List your mentors or coaches. It can be a combination of books, podcasts and persons. It should also include someone who can give you feedback (mentor) or undivided attention for you to dig deep (coach). This enables you to have the fastest learning – from mentors who can guide you to a coach who can support you.

1.
2.
3.
4.
5.

SET ACCOUNTABILITY CHECKPOINTS

Consider the accountability checkpoints you can arrange. E.g. read 1 book a week, meet your coach once a fortnight, or journal every week, etc.

1.
2.
3.

EXERCISE 6.2: DEVELOP YOUR BATTLE PLAN

Remember the clarity score card? I've rephrased it slightly based on what was discussed in earlier chapters.

**DEVELOPING YOUR
B A T T L E PLAN**

remember your clarity score card?

WRITE DOWN YOUR GOAL(S)	DATE

CLARITY OF SELF

How is this aligned to my vision?
Based on the 3Ss Exercise 4.2 (pp117-123), what are the skills I need to get to achieve my goal?
What are the creative ways I can use my strengths to achieve my goal?

CLARITY OF OTHERS

Based on the Client Avatar Exercise 5 (pp136-137), how do I refine and test what my target market wants?

CLARITY OF ACTION

What are the habits I need to have to achieve this goal?
Who are the mentors, coaches or people I need to partner with?
What are the communities I could join?
What are the actions I need to take and the timelines?

Now we review it to develop our battle plan. What are the necessary steps you need to clarify the questions in the table on page 166?

Write the entire list down without judgment; we will categorise them later.

Once you have exhausted your ideas, prioritise them by importance:
- Order it by the most important task first and give yourself a reasonable timeline for each task.
- Are there tasks you can delegate or outsource?

Then, group these action items into immediate one-time action, daily habits, or timed/planned activity. Determine from the list what can be outsourced:

IMMEDIATE:

DAILY/NEW HABITS:

PLANNED:

OUTSOURCED:

I love this as sometimes the goal can seem scary, but once it is broken down into do-able action items, it becomes very achievable. It gives clarity for areas to work on, and it also gives you a section to think about new habits you can create to achieve your goals and to turn your talents into strengths.

Voila! Half the battle is won. Now we've just got to consistently act on it! This is where a coach or a mentor can help.
Accountability helps you to keep yourself on track.

As you create your battle plan, always refer back to Chapter
2, practical steps towards clarity (pp 57-69), to ensure you've
got the necessary foundations in place.

Chapter 7

THE MOST IMPORTANT BATTLE

HOW TO HAVE A LASTING IMPACT ACROSS GENERATIONS

CLARITY CREATES LEGACY

———

"PLEASE THINK
ABOUT YOUR
LEGACY BECAUSE
YOU ARE WRITING
IT EVERY DAY."

Gary Vaynerchuk

WE ONLY HAVE ONE LIFE, ONE GENERATION TO DO WHAT WE can. However, what we do in this life, if we step into our purpose with clarity, can impact generations to come. Never underestimate the impact you can give.

Life is too short to take it easy. So, what happens when we step into our personal authority? Will pride slowly creep in? The most important battle you must conquer is the battle of character. Any structure without a proper foundation will not stand. This is the key to be able to influence across generations.

Character speaks louder than words. People remain in our hearts because of who they are, not because of how successful they are. It's a reminder that as you seek to influence and find authority in this world, you will become a better version of yourself, and not lose yourself through this process.

We can easily measure our skills. However, it's impossible to measure the heart. Your foundation to go higher is really up to you, to your choice of your character.

Whether you like it or not, Adolf Hitler had influence. He had authority. He was able to speak and influence many to war.

However, personal authority without character is manipulation. His influence was only for his generation.

"Leadership is a potent combination of strategy and character. But if you must be without one, be without the strategy." These are the words of General Norman Schwarzkopf, commander of the coalition forces in the Gulf War of 1991. Character is what really matters. It is the only thing that counts in the end.

Let's re-look at the staircase to authority.

THE STAIRCASE TO AUTHORITY

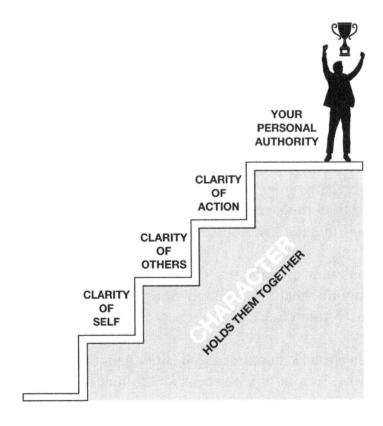

Your character is the foundation of the entire staircase to authority. It is the cement that will hold the steps together and provide an unshakeable base. It will give you the firm and stable foundation to reach way higher than you can ask, think, or imagine, without fearing that you may crash as you go higher.

The greatest influence you have on others is that of your character. Things may change, but if we focus living our lives based on these character principles, they will not fade with time. Your message, your life will pass the test of time. This is how you can have the greatest impact, in the hearts of the people around you, even across different generations.

> Personal authority without character is manipulation.

Be mindful of the values and beliefs you are building as you seek to stand in your authority. Do not let success or busyness take you away from them. Trust is built on character. Trust erodes like how a flower begins to wilt. By the time it is visible that the flower is wilting, it is too late to salvage it. Likewise, invisible attributes like our character need to be constantly fed into all that we do. By the time there is a crack, it will be hard to remedy.

Simon Sinek said:

> *"Trust is maintained when values and beliefs are actively managed. If companies do not actively work to keep clarity, discipline and consistency in balance, then trust starts to break down."*

One of the best ways to stay in character is to remain grateful. It's hard to be proud when we have gratitude. I encourage you to do a gratitude journal. There are a lot of mobile apps nowadays for you to add your grateful notes for the day before you sleep.

Another way is to be dead clear about your values. Work with people you can trust. Be prepared to walk away from transactions or people who have conflicting values. You become who you mix with.

I want to share with you someone who may seem so obscure but had the greatest influence in my life: my nanny.

She was one person who stepped into her own personal authority by embracing who she was, by being faithful to the people around her, and by consistently showing up.

My mum engaged her to look after me when I was born as my mum had to return to work. Even though I'm not blood-related to my nanny, I always considered her my second mum. She earned $200 a month back then to look after me.

She would always share with me stories of her childhood and remind me how lucky I was. When she was young, she wasn't allowed to go to school, because her family could only afford to send the sons to school. She told me that whenever she brought her younger brother to school, she would stand outside the school to learn how to read and write.

She would always tell me she was so grateful they didn't chase her away and she could learn. She had nothing much, but she taught me to be grateful and to persevere, to consistently step towards our goals. I remember she read the Chinese newspapers aloud with pride and with a beautiful grin to show me what she had learnt by herself. I remember she would bring me to buy bread. In the olden days, the traditional bread was burnt brown on the outside and the seller would cut away the skin and sell the bread without the skin. She would buy the bread and ask for the skin too. She gave me the bread and ate the skin. She never complained. She always placed food before me and her children. She taught me we can always choose to be generous, regardless of what we have. Her children have gone on to achieve Masters and start flourishing businesses.

Unfortunately, she passed away when I started writing this book, but she will live on in my heart. Whenever I feel like giving up, I think of her. She gave me permission to dream. In fact, she was my first strengths coach! She taught me to focus on what I have and ignore what I don't have.

She taught me to look beyond the fact that I'm an Asian who speaks with a funny accent, someone who failed English when I was young. She taught me to pursue my dream and **to use what I've got** and not compare. She would always say I was so lucky to be able to go to school. Surely, I would have a lot more opportunities than her. She taught me to count my blessings. It is true. I'm very blessed to have a lot more than her, yet humbly I must learn a lot more to be like her, to learn to use what I've got instead of comparing myself with others. I also aim to pass on her teachings through this book to you.

Clarity begins when we know who we are and accept what we've got. Nanny's the reason why I'm writing this book. I saw her as one who was uniquely wired for greatness by using what she had. She passed away with two successful children and three grandchildren who loved her. Her influence on me will be passed through me to others, to you.

I am very sure you have a lot more opportunities than my nanny. Let's not waste time anymore. Yes, there are battles but if you have the vision, then you have what it takes to achieve it. You can offer to the world only what you have and no one else can do that. You are good enough for you. I am good enough for me. Life is too short for us to compare.

It's choosing to see the gold in you and to work on it to be a better you. I hope that you'll find the gold in you and use what you've got to shine.

Perhaps you know you are different, but you ask yourself, "Do I have anything to offer?" I wrote this book to share with you, just like my nanny, just like Siew May, you do.

It doesn't matter if you believe in God the Creator or not, because as a Gallup Certified Strengths Coach, I am here to share with you this truth - that you are uniquely wired for greatness!

Free yourself. Free yourself from comparison. Free yourself from the expectations of others.

If you are looking for that brightness, that radiance, that glory, that splendour, that clarity, can I encourage you to simply take that first step?

Move past your doubts and step into your destiny.

Because clarity is power, and that power is YOU.

Unleash that power wisely.

I believe in you.

Much love and gratitude,
Ruth

Please note: If you have enjoyed reading this book, I would appreciate if you can offer reviews on Amazon or Goodreads! I would also love to hear from you how this book has helped your journey! Connect with me on social media @ruthsawclarity or write to me through www.ruthsaw.com

Spiritual Clarity

I'm writing this to those who may be interested about how I started my journey to clarity, especially in the area of spiritual clarity. It is my personal journey. I want to be real and authentic to share with you, so there will be references to my faith. Please read on with grace.

I was born in Singapore in the 1970s. Back then Singapore had a 2-child policy. I was unfortunately number three. My mum called me an accident. I found out around the age of 7 that my mum wanted to abort me.

I don't blame her as she had to suffer, and she had no maternity leave, so she left me with my nanny in my early years. On one hand, I felt fortunate to have two mums, my nanny Mondays to Fridays, and my birth mum on the weekends. But at the back of my mind, I felt unwanted. I started my journey seeking clarity, having these questions in my head, "Who am I? Why am I on earth?"

Life continued but things got worse. I was often sick. I used to do well in school, but I got worse as I progressed.

That changed when I came to my faith, when someone told me no, I was not an accident. In fact, he told me God knitted me carefully in my mother's womb, that I was on this earth for a purpose. He told me I was wonderfully and fearfully made (Psalms 139). My friend told me that we are all imperfect, but Jesus came to earth as a perfect man and loved me so much that he chose to die on the cross. He died and paid for my sins and on the third day, he overcame all and rose again. If we put our faith in him, no matter how imperfect we are, we receive his perfectness. Instead of becoming victims of life, we become victorious through him. So, I thought, why not? Why not give it a shot and get to know this Jesus who died on the cross for me?

I began to find hope. I realised this Jesus seems to speak to me through His word, sometimes of correction, sometimes of affirmation, and I felt that warm fuzzy feeling of being loved. Strangely, my health and my studies improved. Life wasn't all smooth sailing and a bed of roses after my faith. I still experienced successes and failures. Through all these, I witnessed miracles and experienced peace, such that I realised this Jesus is alive and fights for me. For example, I found out in my early 20s I had a heart condition and had to visit the cardiologist every year. By the grace of God, I was discharged a few years later after someone prayed for me.

As a Christian, it doesn't mean we don't have troubles. It does mean that we have a God who will lead us forward. My main and foremost clarity is to know that He Himself will lead me in my next step. He who loves me will take care of me. I get to watch my life unfold to things I never thought or believed possible, including writing this book!

The bible declares:

> "For I know the plans I have for you", declares the
> Lord, "plans to prosper you and not to harm you,
> plans to give you hope and a future." Jeremiah
> 29:11 (NIV)

> Jesus himself said "I have come that they may
> have life, and that they may have it more abun-
> dantly." John 10:10 (NKJV)

I pray and wish the same for you. If you are willing to know
this God who led me to my clarity, a day at a time, a step at
a time with love, then say the simple prayer below. Join with
me to believe that indeed you are fearfully and wonderfully
made. Let your Creator guide you to your maximum potential
and open doors that you never thought possible.

The bible says if you confess with your mouth and believe in
your heart that Jesus is Lord, He will come into your heart,
save and guide you (Rom 10:9).

> Dear Lord Jesus, I confess that I do not want to
> live my life on my own. I confess I am imperfect,
> and I need you Lord, a perfect source of light, of
> brightness, of glory and splendour to guide me.
> I open my heart and invite you to come in and
> guide me as my Lord and Saviour.

> Because you chose to die on the cross for me, I
> trust that you will guide me into your goodness
> and into the wonderful destiny and abundant
> life you have prepared for me.

I declare that you are a lamp to my feet, and you will not only guide me each step of the way, you'll also give me the strength to thrive and not just survive.

Thank you, Lord.

In Jesus' Name I pray, Amen.

Congratulations! You are now a believer in Jesus Christ. May I encourage to continue reading His word from the YouVersion Mobile App, attend a Jesus-loving church near you, and attend the Alpha series if the church organises it. I believe God will lead you to places you never felt possible. May the bible verse below, one of my favourite verses, encourage you.

> "The Sovereign Lord is my strength; he makes my feet like the feet of a deer; He enables me to tread on the heights." Habakkuk 3:19 (NIV)

About the Author

Ruth Saw (MBA) is an international bestselling author, speaker and a clarity expert. As a Gallup Certified Strengths Coach, she firmly believes and has witnessed that Clarity is Power. She has spoken to over 2000 people around Australia, New Zealand and Singapore on finding their unique voice.

Having lived and worked in different cultures including the United States of America and Asia Pacific in her consulting practice and corporate career in procurement, she realises that regardless of culture, people will flourish when they know who they are, when they find clarity.

Now Ruth utilises her corporate and coaching experience to enhance organisational and individuals' performance. Through unpacking the strengths of a leader or a team, she helps individuals, organisations and start-ups find their clarity so that they can uncover their potential and flourish.

She herself, found clarity and freedom in pursuing her passion (despite being an introvert!); and now she's dedicated to helping others find their clarity.

Acknowledgements

A big thank you to the following for believing in me and helping me to bring this book to life. There are so many people who have helped me in this journey. If your name is not listed, you know I appreciate you too.

- Austin & Diana Sultana – for being my mentors and my anchor. Thank you for helping me in my entire transition journey to the birth of this book.

- Lorellee & Phil Colley – for being my spiritual mentors. Thank you for speaking words of encouragement over my life.

- Michael Grinder – for mentoring me in speaking and non-verbal communication. When we first met, you told me I love clarity. My heart leapt with a resounding "Yes!" Thank you for your encouragement and for helping me gain clarity to write this book!

- Naomi Deck & Rosa Mai – for your constant prayers, support and friendship.

- Catherine Molloy – for offering me a beautiful space in the farm to write and for helping me structure this book.

- Jessica Kiely & Demian Coorey – for coaching me for my keynote, which gave me insights to refine this book.

- Sam & Kate Cawthorn – for giving me opportunities to pioneer and build the Singapore business for the last 2 years, to speak and hone my craft.

- Warren Tate – for sharing with me on how to launch this book.

- Linda Beaulieu & my brother David Saw – for the detailed editing and proofreading of this book.

- Rosalyn Ng – for the beautiful book cover and the illustrations in the book.

- Marvin Tojos – for the illustrations, immaculate layout and typesetting of the book.

- Tania Waitokia – for encouraging me to start this book-writing journey.

- To my outstanding launch team, friends and family – for your support to launch this book!

Most importantly, I give all praise and glory to my Lord, God the Father, Son and the Holy Spirit. Thank you for guiding and helping me throughout the entire process to create and birth forth this book.

About the publisher, The Clarity Expert

The Clarity Expert (TCE), founded by Ruth Saw, is a faith-based publisher that aims to shine Christ's brightness, radiance, glory and splendour through stories.

TCE believes that true clarity comes from above and seeks to offer authentic and true testimonies to encourage, inspire and motivate. TCE also believes that God can do great things through ordinary broken men and women when we allow our Him to lead and guide.

> "Very truly I tell you, whoever believes in me will do the works I have been doing, and they will do even greater things than these, because I am going to the Father. And I will do whatever you ask in my name, so that the Father may be glorified in the Son. You may ask me for anything in my name, and I will do it."
>
> John 14:12-14 (NIV)

Disclaimer

The material in this publication is for general comment only and does not represent professional advice. It is not intended to provide specific guidance for particular circumstances, and it should not be relied on as a basis for any decision to take action or not take action on any matter which it covers. Readers should obtain professional advice where appropriate, before making such decision. To the maximum extent permitted by law, the author and publisher disclaim all responsibility and liability to any person, arising directly or indirectly from any person taking or not taking action based on the information in this publication.

Made in the USA
Monee, IL
14 November 2020